# How to Advance Through Traffic

Written and Illustrated by Bob Kelton

**How to Advance Through Traffic**

Copyright © 2021 by Robert B. Kelton
Long Beach, CA 90802

Published by Robert B. Kelton

Dedicated to the love of my life,
my **Kathy,**
who has shown great patience
with my need to advance through traffic.

# Table of Contents

# How to Advance Through Traffic

## *Acknowledgments*

The development of this book would have been impossible without numerous contributions from others.  Specifically, I'd like to acknowledge Jim Kelton for his initial advice on having enough speed to pass, for his corrections, and for his numerous content contributions.  A special thank you to Kim Geiser for proofreading my rough draft and to Jason Leiser and Helen Davis for their recommendations on improving the clarity of the text.  I'd also like to thank my wife for her help and support putting this together.

## *Introduction*

In this book we will review the psychology of drivers, driving environments, driving skills and motorist responsibilities. Motorists often behave in seemingly unusual ways. Understanding the underlying psychology will help you understand why other motorists are behaving the way they are. This knowledge will help reduce your stress during your commute.  Various driving environments can cause traffic to behave in predictable ways.  A knowledgeable commuter, using the information in the *Driving Skills* section, can recognize these patterns and advance through traffic.  With all knowledge comes responsibilities.  Take your responsibilities seriously.

Opportunities for advancing through traffic are available at all times.  Using the information contained herein will help you advance through traffic at any time of day.  A significant portion of the text concerns traffic advancement during usual commuting times.  There are two primary reasons for this focus. The first is because the majority of people are most concerned about advancing through traffic during their daily commute and secondly, because a number of situations described occur most frequently during commuting hours.

Most of the scientific work on commuting has been in the area of mental health or productivity.  There is a lot of evidence showing that long commutes can be hard psychologically and physically.  Shortening your commute time is one great way to reduce the harmful effects of commuting.  I've searched and haven't found any actual how-to guides for advancing through traffic.

### Guarantee
Implementing the advice provided here will likely reduce your vehicular commute time by 20%.

The guarantee does not apply to motorcycle commuting.  This is because I have never commuted on a motorcycle.  If you are a motorcyclist, please regift this book to someone who can use it.

### Publication Development
Since I started driving, I have been internally developing methodologies to move though traffic quickly and efficiently. The notes for this document were compiled during actual commutes and started as far back as 1970.

### Illustrations
The illustrations in this publication are not works of art; they are illustrations intended to help illustrate a particular point, so please don't be too critical.


## *Traffic Science*

For years traffic engineers thought that vehicles behaved like particles in a pipe, but observed data didn't support that theory.

Expected bottlenecks didn't always result in a jam and often jams appeared in unexpected locations. The problem with the particle analogy is that particles don't have independent control over their movement as drivers do.

According to Boris S. Kerner, a doctor of physics and mathematics, in his 2004 book *The Physics of Traffic: Empirical Freeway Pattern Features, Engineering Applications, and Theory (Understanding Complex Systems)*, there are three states of traffic. The author identifies them as Free Flow, Synchronized Flow and Moving Jam. The book is technical and covers the complex spatiotemporal aspects of traffic flow. The book is intended for traffic engineers and physicists studying traffic patterns.

Here is a simple summary of the basics of traffic physics: Traffic in a state Free Flow is obviously moving without congestion, but in a state of Synchronized Flow, Dr. Kerner describes the flow as a congested state where the traffic moves a rate slightly below the speed limit, moving large numbers of vehicles in synchronicity. The third state of traffic flow is Moving Jam. In the moving jam, flow is very slow and the traffic is in a high state of congestion. The term "Moving Jam" may be misunderstood as a jam of cars moving slowly together. Actually, the cars move slowly though the jam. It's the jam itself that slowly moves upstream. This is because vehicles approaching the jam slow before they actually reach it and the cars at the front of the jam can accelerate quickly away. This means that major congestion will first appear at a congestion trigger, typically creating synchronized flows before and after the moving jam. Unlike moving jams, synchronized flows remain spatially static and do not migrate in the same way as a moving jam.

I have observed the moving jam on most commutes. When you get through one of these jams and you notice that there isn't an accident or other significant bottleneck, you think, "Why was it congested here?"  It's because the jam has moved upstream from the original bottleneck.

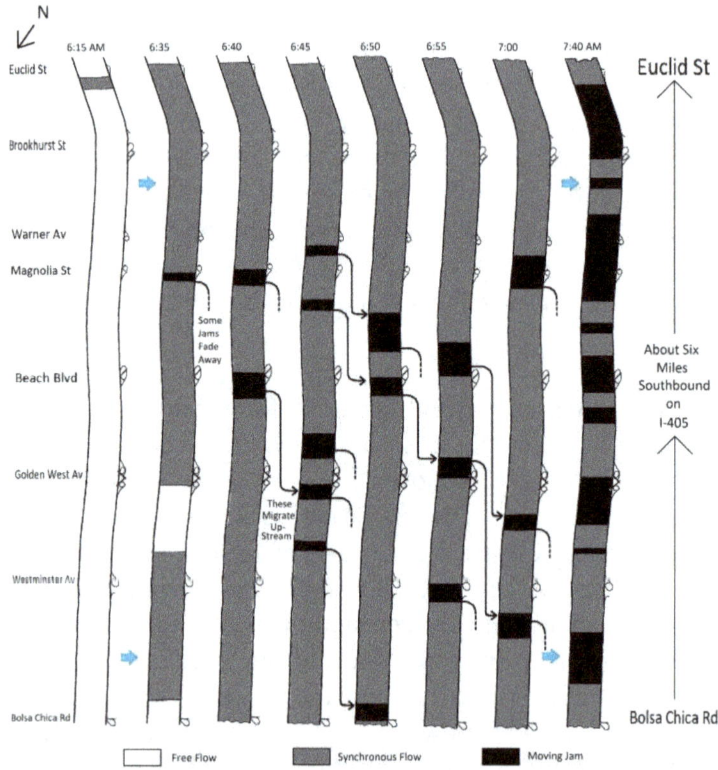


Diagram of the Three States of Traffic Flow – 2003 data

The diagram above is adapted from Dr. Kerner's supporting data.  His data covered a number of international high-traffic locations that all supported his conclusions.  This example from the I-405 freeway in the Los Angeles, California area shows that by 6:35 AM weekdays, there isn't very much free flowing traffic remaining.  And it's gone completely by 6:50 AM.  The diagram illustrates the jams moving upstream.  After 7:00 AM the moving jams, the black areas, expand to as much as 75% of the flow.  During this time frame, the traffic is so congested that the moving jam pattern is no longer evident.  Early in the commute, many of the moving jams dissipate.  After 7:00 AM, most of the moving jams coalesce with others, but still migrate upstream.

Spaciotemporal physics has been difficult to study because accurate data is difficult to obtain.  For the spaciotemporal analysis of traffic, roadway sensors now allow researchers to obtain significantly more data to study.  It's still not enough information to scientifically measure all aspects of traffic dynamics.

An August 2011 "Scientific American" article entitled Crosstown Traffic, by Jennifer Ouellette cited that a team of German scientists in 2004 led by Michael Schreckenberg of the University of Duisberg-Essen, worked to accurately forecast traffic along the autobahn network around Cologne.  They used real-time traffic data from roadway sensors.  The problem with their project was that allowing everyone to know where the congestion was in real-time, caused motorists to modify their behavior.  The drivers rerouted themselves clogging exits and surface streets.  As soon as the motorists modified their routes based upon expected congestion, the models failed.

All of these observations have been at the macro level.  When researchers are able to track each vehicle independently, they will be better able to define accurate traffic models.  This will eventually lead to the validation of the micro traffic dynamics I've observed and am reporting here.


## *My qualifications*

My training in traffic advancement started with my older brother, Jim.  He taught me a number of techniques, such as, that on a two-lane road, I should accelerate to passing speed before moving over to pass.  Over the years, I improved the techniques my brother taught me, and I developed new traffic advancement techniques.  I passed this information on to my cousins, Jan and Curt, and then to my children and niece.  I taught them to drive a number of different vehicles to make sure they were versatile drivers.  I taught them to be very observant and to look for traffic advancement opportunities.  They have all become excellent drivers.

Most people who ride with me say that they are surprised by how quickly we arrived at our destination.  They were not really paying attention to the drive – their right as a passenger – so it is understandable that they did not really notice the drive.  They would have noticed, however, if it was excessively long, rough or jerky.  Those who do pay attention often say, "The traffic just opens up for you."  It is because I am using the techniques described in this book.

**My History of Commuting**

| Years | Destination | Round Trip Miles | Days per week | Number of Years | Total Miles |
|---|---|---|---|---|---|
| 1970-1971 | Swim Practice | 14 | 5 | 2 | 7,000 |
| 1972-1973 | Swim Practice | 40 | 5 | 2 | 20,000 |
| 1973-1978 | University class | 20 | 5 | 5 | 25,000 |
| 1979-1990 | DSA | 35 | 5 | 14 | 125,500 |
| 1991-1992 | ProLogic | 14 | 5 | 2 | 7,000 |
| 1994-1997 | DAI | 14 | 5 | 4 | 14,000 |
| 1998-2004 | AIW | 50 | 5 | 7 | 87,500 |
| 2005-2006 | USAA | 36 | 5 | 2 | 18,000 |
| 2007-2008 | Day Software | 50 | 5 | 2 | 25,000 |
| 2009-2010 | Talend | 50 | 5 | 2 | 25,000 |
| 2012 | SMG | 54 | 5 | 1 | 13,500 |
| 2013-2014 | CA | 20 | 5 | 1 | 5,000 |
| 2015-2019 | Telecommuting |  |  |  |  |
| **Total** |  |  |  |  | **369,500** |

My commuting alone has taken me over 365,000 miles.  At an average of 30 miles per hour (MPH), that's over 12,000 hours in traffic.  If I averaged a speed twice as fast, 60 MPH, my commuting would have taken half of the time, saving over 6,000 hours.  That's the equivalent of working another full-time job for three years.  I haven't yet reduced my commute time 50%, but it is close to 25%.  This is significant.  This is thousands of hours that I've been able to use to do other things rather than sit in traffic.  A lot of time can be saved if you can optimize your commute.

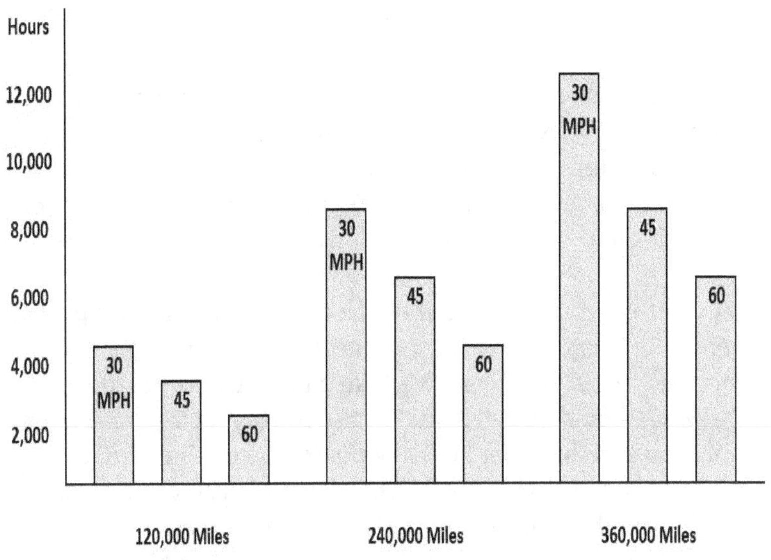


Commuting time savings chart

Most of my commuting time has been during peak commuting volume hours on major commuter routes.  At the peak of commuting congestion, the number of vehicles traveling past a particular point per minute drops significantly because the traffic has slowed.  Theoretically, if the traffic could speed up during peak commuting hours, the volume per hour would increase.

As an example, a 2015 California Department of Transportation study of I-405 traffic volumes in the Los Angeles area showed that vehicles passed Seal Beach Boulevard at the rate of 30,000 vehicles per hour at 7:07 AM.  That works out to about 6,000 vehicles per hour per lane, or 100 vehicles per minute or 1 and 2/3 vehicles per second.  If the average car length is 18 feet and everyone keeps 3.5 car length between them, then:

$$3.5 \times 1\ 2/3 \times 18 = 105 \text{ feet per second}$$
$$105 \times 60 = 6312 \text{ feet per minute}$$
$$6312/5280 = 1.195 \text{ miles per minute}$$
$$1.056 \times 60 = 71.7 \text{ MPH}$$

So, at 7:00 AM traffic would have to maintain a constant rate of speed above 70 MPH in order to handle the large number of vehicles.  Interestingly, at 7:30 the number of vehicles passing the same point drops to only 17,000 vehicles per hour and not surprisingly, the freeway is jammed.

If you remove your car from the freeway for 15 minutes per commute, that's one less car congesting the road for 15 minutes.  If 10,000 drivers were able to do the same, the freeways would be substantially less congested, because not only you and the other 10,000 wouldn't be on the road, the reduced congestion would increase the average vehicle's speed, which gets them off of the road more quickly as well.

The less time you're on the road, the less congestion

I am not recommending that anyone exceed the speed limit or break any other laws, just take advantage of traffic herd mentality.  During a regular commute it is usually difficult to even reach the speed limit.  The techniques outlined in this book will allow you to take advantage of driver's quirks and traffic flow patterns.

I have always tried to use whatever tools were available to optimize my travels.  Now we use Google Maps or Waze and before that people used CB radios.

Many have driven more miles than I, but few, if any, have driven as many miles in as many different commutes.  I've been in every state and more than 25 countries.  I am very observant and have over time developed a set of commuting rules.  Interestingly, these rules tend to apply regardless of where the commute is taking place; even in those countries where they drive on the opposite side of the road.  Please note, these rules are not as applicable to non-commuting drives.  During a regular commute people are focused on their regular destination.  They are not sightseeing (unless there's an accident attracting rubberneckers).

I have extensive commuting experience in Atlanta, Boston, Chicago, Houston, Honolulu, Los Angeles, New York City,

Philadelphia, Phoenix, San Antonio, San Francisco, and Tucson. Although I have commuted in a number of foreign countries, none of them were on a regular basis.

Map showing where I've commuted

**Some specific routes commuted**
I-85 in Atlanta
I-93 in Boston
I-90 in Chicago
I-610 in Houston
H1 in Honolulu
I-405 and Pacific Coast Highway in Los Angeles and Orange County, California
Various roadways in New York City
Schuylkill Parkway and Highway 1 in Philadelphia
I-10 in Phoenix
US 281 in San Antonio
I-80 in San Francisco
Numerous surface streets in Tucson

I-35 W in Minneapolis
I-25 in Denver
I-580 in Livermore


**Extensive commuting in these vehicles:**
1966 Ford Mustang
1973 Ford Pinto
1980 Datsun 310 – manual transmission
1983 Jeep Cherokee Laredo – manual transmission
1986 Jeep Cherokee Laredo – manual transmission
1984 Nissan Sentra – manual transmission
1988 Chevy Lumina
1989 Chevrolet Suburban 2500
1999 Suzuki Esteem – manual transmission
2002 Toyota MR2 Spyder – manual transmission
2004 Ford Escort
2009 Toyota Rav4

Regardless the vehicle I drove, I was always able to advance through traffic efficiently and expeditiously.

## *Psychology of Commuting*

The most critical factor in successfully negotiating a regular commute is to understand the psychology of the average commuter.  Most people on a regular commute are destination oriented and have engaged their autopilot.  They are thinking of other things: What do I need to do at work today?  Do I need to pick-up the kids today?  What do I need to get at the store on the way home tonight?

A number of commuters are actively trying to expedite their drive, but without understanding how the other drivers will behave, they get stuck after taking unnecessary risks.  This tends to make them wary on future commutes and they return to being unobservant and timid.  Once you familiarize yourself with the principles in this guide, you'll readily identify the basic psychological commuting patterns.

There are subconscious driving patterns at all times, but the most consistently identifiable patterns are during commuting hours and late at night.  The patterns during the morning commute are the most consistent.  After the morning commute, a wide variety of non-commuting drivers join the roadways. Appointments, deliveries, shopping, visiting, sightseeing plus a thousand other activities occupy the purposes of the drivers entering the roadway after 9:30 AM weekdays.  Many of the drivers are going someplace new or on a route they don't drive frequently.  This leads to more congestion than would occur with the same number of vehicles during a typical morning commute.  Most of these non-commuting drivers try to get off the roads before the afternoon rush hours, but there are enough remaining to slow the afternoon commute.  It only takes one careless lane change to cause a cascading slowdown in the traffic behind them.  Physics author, Boris S. Kerner, wrote that local random traffic perturbations such as a careless lane change, are the catalyst for the generation of a jam.  For an afternoon commuter, the illusion of fast-moving traffic is quickly dashed by one careless lane change.  This increases the number of extremely frustrated commuters trying to get home quickly – a common cause of "road rage."  If you want to be a victim of road rage, merge in front of another driver and then slow down. That angers drivers as much as anything else.  Avoid road rage by learning how other drivers behave, and use their behavior to your advantage.

## *Understanding the Commute*

There are a wide variety of ways to commute.  Some walk; some ride a bicycle; some take taxis or, rideshare services such as Uber and Lyft, some take helicopters or airplanes, some take subways, ferries, buses, trains, light rail or aerial tramways.  But most need to include travel by personal vehicle during some portion of their commute.  Perhaps they take a car to the train station or to the airport.  Of all of the commuting methodologies, the one with the greatest individual control is the commuter who drives.  Most of this guide is to assist you in optimizing the driving aspect of your commute.

**Define your commute**
Where do you have to go?
How far is it?
When do you need to be there?
How long do you need to be there?
Are your hours flexible?
How often do you need to be there?
Are there other locations involved?
Are there other commuting options?
Does your employer have a van option?
Is a carpool available?

**Know your vehicle**
How long is it?  Can you tell how close you are to another vehicle?  Practice by going to a large empty parking lot and pull your vehicle up to a light post or other similar object and make sure you can pull all of the way up to it without touching; both forwards and backwards.  Get out multiple times and verify the distances.  Do this for all of the vehicles you drive.  It is critically

important that you know the full characteristics of your vehicle. Visibility varies dramatically on each vehicle, so learn everything you can about the handling of your ride.  Adjust your mirrors to cover blind spots, not to see your vehicle.  There is specific advice available online to help you adjust your mirrors for optimal visibility.

Driver checking the distance between his car and a light pole

Have a location for all of your stuff.  You don't want to search under your seat for your phone while driving.  Get a mount for your phone and use Waze, or other navigational application for your smartphone.  Use a Bluetooth earbud with your phone so you can operate it handsfree.  Get a good radar detector.  Get a dash camera (dash cam) to protect yourself in the event of an accident.  (If it happens to be your fault, swallow the SIM card.) Make sure everything has the appropriate power cord.

## *The Psychology of Drivers*

As discussed in the section on the psychology of commuting, understanding how the other drivers will behave is the basis for effective commuting.  Observe the other drivers around you. Most vehicles are likely to be driven by a driver with a particular style.  For example, if stereotypes prevail, a minivan will probably be driven by a conservative soccer mom and a contractor's pickup truck by an impatient construction supervisor.  Remember though, the real factor is not the vehicle, but the driver.  Smokers tend to drive fast and young mothers tend to drive slowly.  The drivers of old poorly maintained cars are usually slow.  At a traffic light, late model buses and commercial trucks are generally fast off the line – don't be afraid of using the shortest lane when there is a late model bus or truck that lane.

Notice the gap drivers leave between themselves and the vehicle in front of them.  Tailgaters are likely impatient and drive too close to the vehicle in front of them, in hopes that they'll accelerate.  The driver in front is usually distracted by the tailgater and will start watching them instead of watching the road.

Observe where other drivers are looking.  Are they blankly looking down the road or talking on their phone?  Determine the type of drivers around you as you advance through traffic. Compare their types to the driver profiles below.


## Driver Profiles

Every driver behaves like each of these profiles at some point. Don't get hung up on the profile name; it's just an identifier of a particular driving style.  The driver profiles are much easier to remember by using the typical profile descriptor assigned to them here.  Avoid tailing profiles with an asterisk (*) because they are either habitually slow or because they drive erratically. On the other hand, it may be wise to follow some of the profiles marked with a plus sign (+) because they often open passing lanes in traffic.  Once they execute a merge, the trailing car will often back off even more, providing you with a large opening in which to merge.

The driver profiles are ordered by the likelihood of encountering them on your daily commute.

**Office Worker Male**
Merges occasionally trying to advance, but spends most of the commute in the same lane driving the usual route.

**Office Worker Female**
Typically stays in a specific lane most every day.  Is used to the same pattern and won't vary much, especially during the morning commute.

**Tailgater***
Tailgaters are of two types.  Habitual tailgaters and impatient tailgaters.  Habitual tailgaters have learned bad driving habits and need to improve their driving skills.  Impatient tailgaters have someplace to be and the traffic is frustratingly slow.  They drive too close to the vehicle in front of them hoping that they'll accelerate.  Unfortunately, the driver in front rarely has any room to move forward, so when he slows (even when he doesn't brake), the tailgater has to hit his brakes.  This usually causes a cascade of braking behind them.  (See "Cascading Braking" in the *Driving Environments* section.)  It's okay to merge in front of one of these drivers.  They will likely honk and then tailgate you, but they won't hit you.  I try not to merge behind them because they will constantly hit their brakes.  I give them extra distance, so I don't need to hit my brakes every time they tap theirs.  It's like they're sending Morse code, dot-dot-dash-dash-dot-dash-dot.

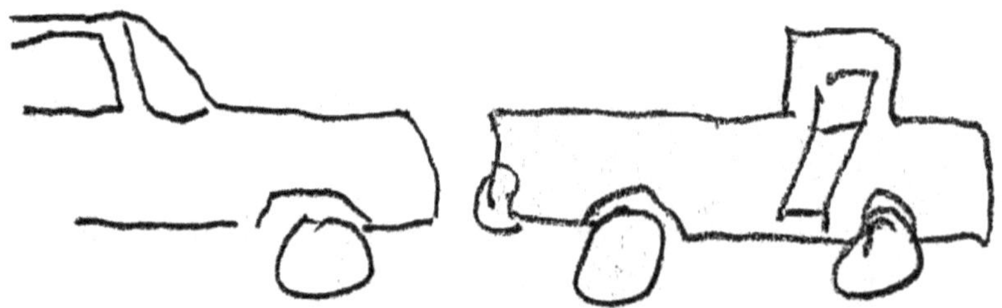

Tailgaters are annoying

People driving vans tend to tailgate more than most people. This is because they sit so far forward that they feel like there's plenty of room.  Actually, they are at more risk in a collision because there is significantly less crumple zone in their vehicle to absorb an impact.  A van driver's consistency in tailgating, makes them fall into the habitual tailgater category.

**Delivery Truck Driver**
Destination oriented.  They are usually predictable and not aggressive.  They often know the route well.  If you see the same delivery trucks often, you'll notice they usually stay in the lanes that advance most predictably.

**Semi-tractor Trailer Driver**
Destination oriented.  Unless turning, they usually stay in the right lanes.  On freeways they usually occupy the second lane from the right.  Most commuters avoid this lane because they assume the trucks are slow and dangerous. These highly observant drivers usually advance against traffic at a consistent rate because all of the commuters avoid the "truck lanes."  See more in the "Traffic Accordions" section.

Be aware of heavily loaded trucks.  They will move very slowly off the line from a traffic light.

**Buses**

Be observant in your local area.  City buses now accelerate faster than in the past, moving quickly off the line at traffic lights.

**Salespeople**

Always late.  Always impatient.  Often on the phone and distracted.  They can be fast at times, but are inconsistent.  A cross between their handsfree talking and their stylish late model luxury vehicle will help you identify this driving profile.

**Construction Supervisor+**

Needs to get to the construction site now.  Usually aggressive and impatient.  They are usually observant and their traffic experience often allows them to advance through traffic effectively.

**Rubbernecker***

This is a temporary affliction, often affecting otherwise effective drivers.  These drivers adversely affect thousands of motorists and can extend a commute by an hour.  Be careful: They can appear spontaneously almost anywhere.  No matter the event, you should never rubberneck or sightsee because you are the driver.  If you want to look, exit the roadway.

Rubberneckers are dangerous – don't be one

## Soccer Mom*
Doesn't want to be in traffic.  If she is a regular commuter, she will likely drive like the Office Worker Female.  Otherwise, she'll probably drive like the Elderly Driver.

## Entitled Driver*
Once they are in a lane, it is their right to be there.  They are also often afraid to change lanes.  This driver tends to clog the left lanes.  This profile is often found in conjunction with one of the other profiles.

## Landscaping Truck Driver*
Usually slow and inattentive.

Drivers of landscaping trucks are usually slow

## Drivers with Disabilities

Drivers with disabilities, often identifiable by a special plate or placard, are not necessarily slow drivers, so don't judge them too quickly.  Assess their traffic responses to determine which other driving profile may actually fit their driving style.  There are other considerations when driving near these drivers.  A few examples:

- Their vehicle may have hand controls and they may be able to stop faster than an able-bodied driver.  Why is that?  People in wheelchairs likely won't be using their feet for accelerating and braking.  Their hand may be on a push/pull mechanism that controls both braking and accelerating.  These drivers won't need to take their foot off of the gas pedal to move it to the brake.
- Some drivers may have one hand on the steering wheel and the other on the push/pull control.  Because the

driver is using both hands, the driver's ability to look over either shoulder is limited.  Be more aware of the driver's limited visibility when passing vehicles with a disability plate.

- Note: When parking, do not park close to the blue line of a designated disability space.  If you are on the line, you can be cited.  Also, many people with disabilities need extra space for their wheelchairs when entering and exiting their vehicles.  You don't want your car doors scratched because you parked too close to the handicapped space. Plus, it's inconsiderate.

**Elderly Driver*** – if not covered elsewhere in another category above

Usually a very slow and cautious driver.  Many of these drivers have vision issues, making them uncomfortable in traffic.  They often try to avoid freeways because they are afraid to make lane changes, are concerned about congestion, or worried that the traffic will move too fast.

**Angry or Erratic Driver***

The angry driver has recently gotten some bad news or has had something bad happen.  It doesn't matter what it is.  Avoid these drivers.  They are erratic and will change lanes carelessly.  It is unlikely that they are angry at you; they are angry with their current situation.  Other erratic drivers may be distracted or might be inebriated and are very dangerous.  They are unpredictable.

Examples:
Angry Driver - remote Arizona
An angry driver between Why (yes, it's an actual town in Arizona) and Sells, Arizona.  On remote Arizona Highway 86, in the middle of the desert near midnight, I passed what looked like three guys in a pickup truck. There was no one on the road so it was an easy rural

pass with plenty of room to spare in my 4-liter Jeep Cherokee.  This is in the middle of Tohono O'odham Indian Reservation.  For dozens of miles in every direction there is nothing.  No lights.  No Traffic.  I maintained my prior overtaking speed, which is usually enough for a passed vehicle to maintain their prior speed.  This guy accelerated abruptly and came right up on my tail.  We were going 70 mph (in a 55 zone) and this guy was right on me and wasn't looking to pass.  It was a very bad location for a road confrontation (actually, all places are bad for a road confrontation), so I didn't want to stop.  I accelerated and he did too.  He stayed right on me.  The road transitioned from a straight shot to hilly curves.  I kept up my speed and he had great difficulties driving 90 on the curves.  I moved steadily away from him until he was no longer visible.  I didn't want there to be any chance of him catching up with me again, so I increased my speed to 105 on the next long straight-away.  We drove through some other hills and I felt like I had lost him.  And like some horror movie, on the next long stayaway I could see his headlights approaching in the distance.  I increased my speed to 105 again and he was still approaching.  He was gaining steadily on me, but after 20 minutes we again came to an area with hills and I was able to lose him finally.  Fortunately, I never saw him again.

Erratic Driver – near Lake Pleasant, Arizona
One late afternoon, we had a similar experience with a guy near Lake Pleasant north of the Phoenix area.  Once I passed him, he behaved like a maniac.  I had no place to exit, so I used the same technique as above to evade him.  I'd get a good lead on him and then he'd come barreling back.  I was eventually able to get away from him, but he made us very uncomfortable.

Erratic Motorcyclist – I-8, rural California
On a clear morning, eastbound between Ocotillo,
California and Yuma, Arizona, a distance of about 85
miles, we encountered a motorcyclist who was driving
erratically on I-8.  At times, he was hanging over his
handlebars like he wanted to take a nap.  He was
dragging his foot on the pavement at 70 mph.  He was
changing lanes without any apparent reason.  He would
drive fast and then would slow down.  We passed him
and then he passed us.  We were using cruise control,
so our speed was constant.  We passed him again and
then he passed us again.  He slowed a lot and we
passed him again.  We mistakenly thought we had
gotten away from him.  Then suddenly he sped past us
and slowed to our speed.  This pattern went on for half
an hour.  He wasn't threatening to us, but his erratic
behavior was annoying and dangerous, and we didn't
want to join him in an accident.  We were finally able to
pass him for good when we were able to maneuver
though some traffic and he got stuck behind a truck.

## Macho Driver

Typically, a guy who doesn't want to be passed.  Most drivers
don't want to be passed, but this profile hates to be passed and
will repass you at the earliest opportunity.  Eventually he gets
distracted, until you go to pass him again.  Perseverance will
eventually get you around this guy.

## Observant Drivers+

Amazingly there are some out there.  Follow them as long as
they are useful.  Most are only truly observant for short periods
of time.  Usually, they fall back into one of the other driver
types.

This is the Driver Profile I try to emulate.  If everyone drove as an Observant Driver, traffic would move smoothly and safely.

**Cement Truck Driver***
Always slow to start and usually slow on the road.  Unlike most other vehicles, the driver of this vehicle isn't as important as the vehicle itself.  This applies for all extra heavy trucks.

**Inconsiderate Driver***
Fortunately, there are not very many of these drivers, but still some drivers delight in closing passing/merging opportunities. It may take a few more minutes than usual, but pass them to avoid them.

## Subconscious Driving Patterns

In addition to the driver profiles, drivers also have subconscious driving patterns.  Everyone is subject to the effects of these subconscious patterns.  Observe your own behavior related to these patterns and try to avoid their lure.

**Subconscious Overtaken Reaction**
Drivers being overtaken usually speed up to match the passing vehicle.  This is a subconscious act.  You may have noticed it yourself when someone goes to pass you.  You suddenly notice that you've accelerated to the speed of the passing motorist. When you go to pass, the driver you're passing perceives your movement and subconsciously accelerates.  Once passed, they slow down, often after looking at their speedometer, realizing they're going faster than they want to drive.  You can overcome this reaction by passing quickly.  Sometimes I'll even slow my pass a little until my front bumper is even with their back door and then accelerate to complete the pass quickly.  The sudden pass reduces the subconscious reaction.

### Subconscious Slow Pass Reaction

When a passing motorist advances next to the vehicle being passed, the passing driver often slows to the speed of the vehicle being passed.  When you couple this reaction with the subconscious overtaken reaction cited above, you'll often get two vehicles driving side-by-side for a long distance.  This is a complete blocker for anyone behind when there are only two lanes available.

### Subconscious Merge Reaction

Motorists in adjacent lanes usually don't notice when you've aligned yourself for a merge.  If you follow the suggestions in the section on merging, you'll notice that if you merge with confidence, the trailing motorists in your new lane will subconsciously slow a little.  Take advantage of this reaction to facilitate smooth merges.

### Go Fast and Then Slow

Some drivers pass and appear to be moving quickly, advancing through traffic and then suddenly they stall in traffic for no apparent reason.  This pattern is usually driven by a recent event on the road.  Someone "cuts them off," and they need to get back into the flow.  Or they see another driver advancing through traffic and they want to emulate their success.  After a few minutes they get distracted and stall in traffic.

### Leader of the Pack

A driver who feels like they are the one finding traffic advancement opportunities will often drive much more aggressively than they would usually.  This occurs spontaneously whenever the traffic has a decent movement to it.  The feeling of being the leader of the pack is exhilarating and they may continue regular traffic advancement for their entire commute.  Look in the sub-section Leader of the Pack in the *Driving Skills* section for advice on how to encourage this feeling in other motorists.

### False Sense of Slowing

When a motorist notices a vehicle advancing from behind, they will instinctively think that they've slowed.  If they have room, they'll automatically accelerate a bit.

### Standard Start Gap

After coming to complete stop, drivers will wait for the vehicle in front of them to start moving, usually about 2 seconds, before moving themselves.  Drivers of trucks may wait 3 or 4 seconds before they start moving.  This is a subconscious act. Most motorists won't notice how much gap they leave before starting unless the vehicle in front of them is slow to start moving.

This leads to a Driving Principle: The longer a lane has been moving slowly, the more compressed it becomes and the longer it will take proportionally to decompress.

## Conscious Driving Patterns

Conscious driving patterns can be exhibited by any of the driver profiles.  The driver profiles cover basic behavior, this section covers some of the conscious driving patterns you will encounter.

### Usual

The vast majority of commuters when they are paying attention, try to be courteous.  They allow a zipper merge, when necessary, and they try to avoid causing issues for other motorists.

### Psychopathic

Out of 100 people, one will be psychopathic. On the road there are hundreds of drivers, so a few will be psychopathic.  Some seem to delight in annoying other drivers.  Just realize that, occasionally, there will be someone who wants to annoy everyone.  Just try to work your way around them.  If they are scaring you, use the "Exit Strategy" described in the *Driving Skills* section.

**Righteous Driver**
A Righteous Driver believes it is his or her responsibility to make you conform to their definition of "correct driving."  When they see you are going to overtake them, they intentionally make it difficult.  They think, "Hey, I'm stuck here in traffic – you should be stuck too."  This driver will delight in cutting you off if they think you are driving recklessly.  This is the same driver who would move to the left lane and drive below the speed limit to slow everyone else.

**Advancing Through Traffic**
Advancing though traffic is infectious.  As other motorists see you moving through traffic, they'll consciously want to advance with you.  They will often abandon their usual driving profile and adopt the observant driver profile.  Suddenly you realize that you have a trail of other drivers following you through traffic.  Focus on your advancement, they will usually give you room and priority for merges.  If someone advances past you, follow them.  Team passing will generate a larger number of traffic advancement opportunities.


## Your Psychology

Practice conscientious and effective driving skills until they become your habit.  At traffic lights, leave enough room to see the tires of the car in front of you or if you're the lead car at the light, make sure you can see all of the crosswalk – don't encroach on the pedestrian's right of way.

Your commute is not a race.  Every day you will need to deal with a new set of circumstances that will improve your driving skills.  The goal is to optimize your travels.

There are times you may need to be assertive.  Drivers nearby may not understand who has the right-of-way at various times.  The indecision will cause everyone to wait.  Sometimes you just need to assert your right-of-way or take the right-of-way if no one else will.

Some drivers optimize their commute by listening to audiobooks or podcasts.  There's nothing wrong with this as long as you are maintaining your observance of the traffic.  Audiobooks are especially great for cross-country drives, but the stories may lose continuity when heard during a commute.

Some make phone calls to optimize their commuting time.  This can also be okay as long as you remain observant.  I've taken many calls while commuting.  Sometimes it's unavoidable, but I recommend against this practice as much as practical.  I noticed, that several times I got very involved in the call and nearly had an accident.  I rarely take calls while driving now.

In car distractions will seriously impair your driving effectiveness.  Whether it's fumbling with fast food or your child in the backseat, distractions can end your life.  Stay focused on the task of driving effectively.


## *Driving Environments*

Most drivers deal with city traffic, freeways, and inclement weather on a regular basis during their commutes.  In any one commute it's likely that you'll encounter a number of these driving environments.  The environments include both physical environments such as freeways and traffic lights, but also includes certain driving patterns and behaviors that create driving environments during the commute.  The following environments are ordered by the environments you're most likely to encounter.


## City Multi-Lane Roads

City multi-lane roads have at least two lanes going in your direction. In most locales, these roadways have nearly unlimited access and have frequent intersections.  This is the most common commuting environment.  Frequent traffic lights and lots of motorists entering and exiting from a multitude of directions often causes the traffic in this environment to crawl. Observe the flow and patterns of your commute.  There are many opportunities to advance through traffic in this environment.  See the advice in the *Driving Skills* section, particularly in the sub-sections on "Merging," "Accordion Opportunities," and "Traffic Lights."

Don't hit the brakes for every car approaching your throughway. They will stop.  They've been approaching this intersection every day and they know they'll need to stop or at least yield the right-of-way.  Maintain your speed and don't tap your brakes.

This driving environment often includes a large number of pedestrians.  As mentioned elsewhere, don't encroach on crosswalks and remember some pedestrians need extra time to cross.  Be very careful passing a car stopped at a crosswalk, a pedestrian you can't see may be crossing the street.  Be observant for cyclists riding on the sidewalk.  By riding on the sidewalk, they are showing a lack of consideration for pedestrians.  They are also putting their own safety at risk since bicycles moving quickly on a sidewalk are not clearly visible to vehicles turning left across the crosswalk.

Multi-lane city road – commercial area with lots of cross-traffic

## Traffic Lights

One of the most common sights for a regular commuter.  Be
very observant at traffic lights.  It is the most likely place for a
serious accident to occur.  Be observant also for the patterns in
the traffic at each light.  Lights are not at all the same.  Some
will give priority to vehicles turning left or for vehicles going
north.  Observe and log the patterns around the traffic lights on
your commute.

## Freeway - City

The freeway – city environment is complex.  The human caused driving environments – traffic accordions and cascading braking – are on full display on city freeways.  Much of the information contained herein will help you navigate this complex environment.  As a general rule, the second lane from the right will usually move little faster than adjacent lanes in heavy traffic.

Additional information is provided in the *Driving Skills* section, "Advancing Through Traffic," for dealing with this driving environment.

## Cascading Braking

Occurs when a driver sees brake lights in front of him and hits his brakes in an automatic response.  I've seen it cascade for a mile because of one driver merging at an inopportune time.

From one set of brakes in the distance the cascade starts

The cascade flows through the drivers

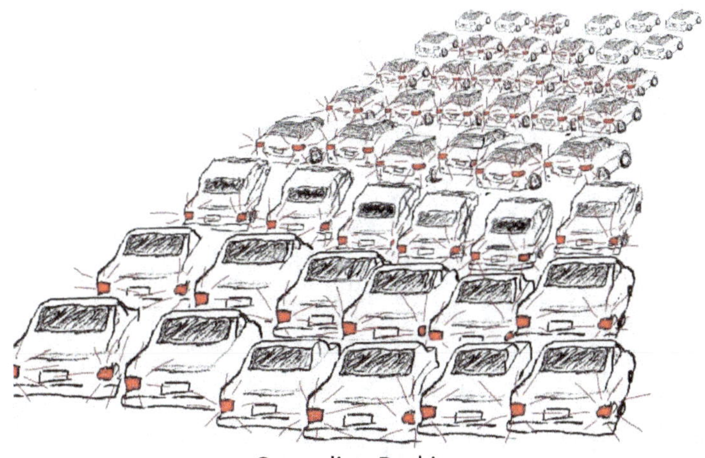

Cascading Braking

## Traffic Accordions

This phenomenon occurs regularly in heavy traffic.  At lights, near accidents or construction zones, or at any point where the traffic slows significantly, the traffic will compress.  Once past the light/accident/construction zone/etc., each driver will typically let the vehicle in front of them move away (the opening of the accordion).  This is why a truck or bus will move quickly after a bottleneck because it doesn't need intermediary gaps.  Most drivers wait for a count of about two seconds before they move (the standard traffic gap) after the light changes or the vehicle in front of them moves.  This is a cascade through each vehicle.  So, for each vehicle, multiply by two seconds to get an estimated move time.  To a lesser degree than at a light, accident or construction zone, ordinary traffic can spontaneously create traffic accordions, so look for them and use them to advance.  Note where these occur regularly on your daily commute.

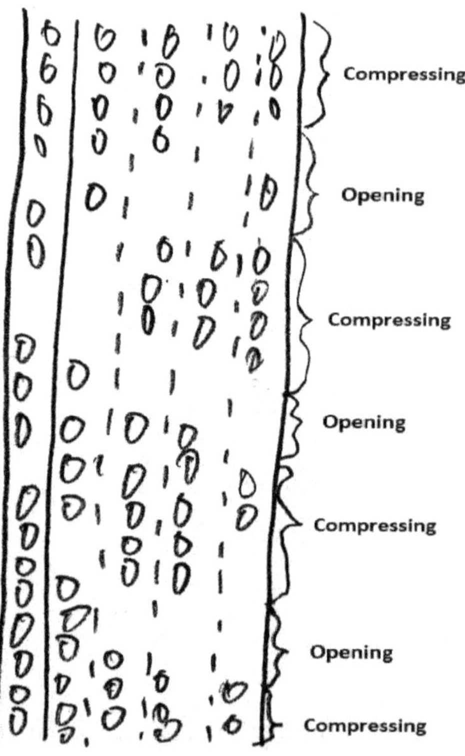


Traffic accordions create traffic advancement opportunities

## Cyclists and Motorcyclists

As a cyclist, I'm sympathetic to other cyclists.  When I encounter
one during a commute, I hope that they'll ride predictably and
will follow the local cycling laws.  Most commuting cyclists will
avoid narrow roads where there isn't enough room for a vehicle
to easily pass without coming within three feet.  Most states
have a statute specifying the minimum passing clearance
required.  This is usually three feet, but please pass with a wider
berth.  You can easily identify the experienced cyclists; they
behave confidently and predictably in traffic and will not
interfere when you need to pass.  They expect it.

Be especially careful when approaching an inexperienced cyclist
when commuting.  You can usually identify the less experienced
cyclists, some will weave, some will look back fearfully and
others will clearly not be focused on their ride.  If possible,
merge a lane to the left to give them extra room.

Be conscious of cyclists and motorcyclists on the road.  At traffic
lights, leave room for cyclists to pass you on the right as they
move all of the way up to the light.

In some states, motorcyclists are allowed split lanes, meaning
they can ride the white line between vehicles.  In these states,
you'll sometimes have a loud motorcycle pass between you and
an adjacent vehicle in traffic.  It has made me jump.  Some
drivers get angry with the passing motorcyclists, but the good
thing is that they are not further clogging the roads, so in
actuality your commute is shorter.  Don't trap a motorcyclist
next to you by riding the dotted line.  Riding midway between
the lines will provide enough room for a motorcyclist to easily

pass next to you and will reduce the likelihood that another driver drifting out of his lane will tag you.

## Weather

Icy roads are extremely hazardous even for experienced drivers and should be avoided if possible.  Flooding presents very different challenges.  Areas that are usually dry can become lakes.  Driving in extremely hot conditions can be very dangerous as well.  If you break down on the side of the road in Phoenix when the shade temperature is above 120 degrees Fahrenheit (>48 degrees Celsius), you could die before roadside assistance arrives.  Temperatures are always taken in the shade, so the measurement is of the air.  If the air temperature is 120 degrees, the temperature of the pavement will be above 160 degrees (71 degrees C).  Your dashboard could be 180 (82 C).

On a hot day in Tempe, Arizona, I came across a pedestrian who had gotten hit in a crosswalk.  The onlookers had left him on the scorching hot pavement until the paramedics arrived.  The paramedics were livid at the gawkers, telling them that the burns he received lying on the hot pavement were more likely to kill him than the accident itself.  The fellow did live but had second degree burns, with blisters, wherever he had been in contact with the pavement.  Don't underestimate the dangers of heat.

## Freeway - Rural

Usually these freeways have two lanes in each direction with limited access ramps and no cross traffic.  Amazingly, in remote rural areas, people will line up in long lines in the left lane to pass a slightly slower vehicle ahead.  Stay right to pass all of the vehicles in the left lane – an easy merge option will nearly always appear.

Use the guidance provided in the *Driving Skills* section, "Freeway – Rural," for additional information on dealing with this driving environment.


## Highway - Rural

Rural highways have their own dynamics.  Study the traffic patterns on your drives.  Certain road conditions are far more common on rural roads.  For example, most breaking should be done before you enter a curve, but most motorists apply their breaks through the turn.  The intense physical pressure on the road by numerous vehicles will cause waffling in the pavement. You will notice in these curves, the unevenness of the pavement by the shaking of the steering wheel.  Rural roads are far more likely to have serious pavement defects, so be alert.


## Toll roads

Generally, there are two types of toll operations, those that are required, like bridge tolls, and those that are used to bypass traffic.  This guide is most concerned about the toll roads used for expediting travel.  Some people love toll roads because it saves them time and relieves most of the stress related to commuting in heavy traffic.  These tolls mount up and many people pay $400 or more per month for these tolls.  If you're too frugal to pay these tolls, as I am, follow this guide to significantly reduce your commute time, without needing to pay high tolls.

## Traffic Circles

Traffic circles or roundabouts are very popular in Europe where roads were designed around old walking paths.  In ancient times, roads used to lead to courtyards and plazas in cities.  When more than two roads intersect, a standard traffic light intersection doesn't move traffic efficiently.  A traffic circle will allow a continuous stream of traffic to enter and exit without having any direct cross traffic or left turns (for drivers driving on the right) in front of traffic.  This design reduces serious accidents because all of vehicles are going in the same direction.  Also, vehicles already in the traffic circle have the right of way over vehicles entering.

## Reversable Lanes

Some communities have reversable lanes.  Some of these are controlled by lights, some by gates, and others by cones.  In all cases, the concept is to add additional temporary lanes to the primary direction of commuter travel.  Many commuters are reluctant to use these lanes.  Some call them suicide lanes.  It gives them an excuse for not using them.  The lanes are often less dangerous than the other lanes.  I recommend using them whenever the lanes are advancing.

Reversable lanes activated for my direction

Reversable lanes activated for oncoming traffic

## *Driving Skills*

Practice the skills listed here every time you drive.  Be courteous but take advantage of openings in the traffic.  Use your skills to advance through traffic.  It's a process.  Usually you'll advance, but sometimes you'll lose ground.  Be patient.  It's a probability game.  Play the odds.

The driving skills are arranged in order of how important each is to most commuters.

## Vehicle Operation

Review the owner's manual.  If you don't have it, you can usually find them online.  Follow the recommended maintenance schedule.  Don't skimp on maintenance.  The longevity, dependability and performance of your vehicle is directly related to the care you put into maintaining it.   Walk around your vehicle before every drive to make sure everything looks right.  You'll often spot potential issues long before they become problems, allowing you to deal with them easily.

Become an expert at operating your vehicle.  Understand the capabilities of your vehicle, how it will handle in various environments.  Practice on ice and in water.  Practice steering into the skid when the vehicle hydroplanes.  Make it a habit to react correctly.

There are driving schools that allow you to bring your car to their test tracks.  You can improve your driving skills in the car you'll be driving regularly.  A number of my friends swear by these.

## Observation

The most important thing anyone can do to improve their commute is to not get stuck in avoidable situations.  Observation is the most important tool available to you during your commute.  By observing your vehicle, you avoid breakdowns.  By observing the reactions of the drivers ahead, you can determine evasive actions well before the other drivers around you even realize that they need to take action.  Just as an experienced sailor can read the wind, an observant commuter can read the traffic.

Watch well ahead.  Scan as far up the road as possible.  Look through the windshield of the car in front of you.  Watch for vehicles approaching from side streets and anticipate what they will do.  Watch the car in front of your car for braking and accelerating cues.  As you commute, observe the flow of traffic in the other lanes.  Is there a pattern?  Usually there is.  Observe that on multi-lane roads, people turning right rarely turn into the right-most lane.

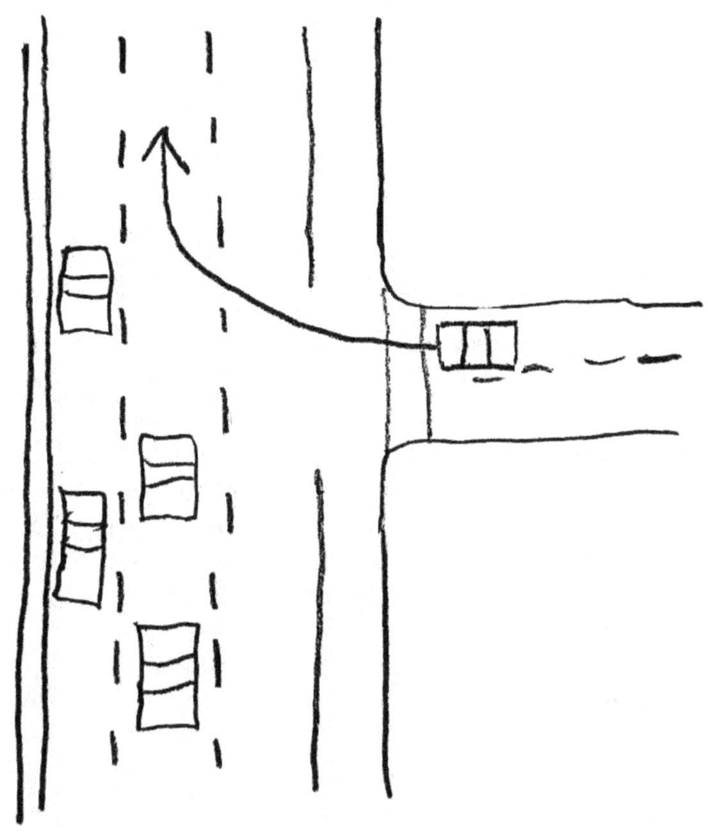

Right turner into middle lane

Look for brake lights anywhere in front of you.  Braking is
usually a sign that someone ahead is not merging correctly.
Observe the usual braking patterns on different stretches of
your commute and determine alternate routes if the pattern
seems abnormal.

If you get too close to large vehicles, your long-range view can
be completely obstructed.  Driving in the right lanes on
freeways is usually faster than in the left lanes, but if there are a

lot of trucks, your long-range visibility may be hampered to the point that traffic situations materializing in front of you might get you temporarily trapped.  Try to maintain visibility even when trying to take advantage of regular traffic patterns.

## Planning

Plan your routes and make sure you've identified alternate routes.  Even if it's twice as long, make sure you have an alternate route.  One year in Phoenix, flooding rains closed most of the bridges across the Salt River during the middle of a work day.  The Salt River runs through the middle of the Phoenix metro area and the bridge closings stranded people on the wrong side of the river for four days.  Some people discovered that the Amtrak rail bridge was open and by abandoning their cars, they were able to cross by rail for several more hours until it was closed as well.  Others took highways more than a hundred miles out of their way to circumvent closed and washed out bridges.  All of these bridges were later closed, cutting the city in half for several days.

Plan on having more fuel than you need for any particular drive. Typically, you should refill at about half a tank.  If you do, you'll never need to make an emergency fill-up.  Carry water and some sort of food items.  Protein bars are a good option.  I use stainless steel for the water bottles in my vehicle.  They won't leach chemicals into the water, even on very hot days.

Explore and tune alternate routes so you can reroute if there's a major accident.  I recommend an application like Waze for getting real-time alternate route recommendations.  It can alert you to the locations of accidents, objects in the road, the police and road construction.  Make sure you've done your due diligence and don't rely exclusively on a GPS system for rerouting.  Sometimes these applications just won't work.  Also,

GPS application route time estimates use the current traffic volume for time calculations.  As congestion increases, these estimates can extend dramatically.  On a daily basis, compare the GPS system's time estimate to your actual commute duration.

An additional word of caution when using GPS apps for rerouting.  Previously, I mentioned a "Scientific American" article on traffic.  Researchers have discovered that when people reroute, they can clog the alternate routes faster than the traffic models can predict the changing traffic congestion.  I usually take the rerouting suggestions, but if the rerouting seems unusual, I'll review the jam location.  Sometimes I'll avoid the reroute if the jam is short or the reroute seems likely to congest.

If you are running late, be extremely cautious taking an unverified alternate route, even if it is recommended by your GPS app.  It will almost always take more time than expected.  If you've pre-vetted this alternate route, then you know what to expect and you can proceed.

Plan to get large gains at predictable points at various sections of your commute.  Plan your commute so you can optimize it. Commute at different times to find the best times for your commute.  Be as flexible as possible.  Check both in the early morning and later in the evening.  Optimize your commute by combining trips.  An afternoon side trip can often accomplish some errand for you and allow traffic to clear a bit before restarting your commute.


## Merging

For effective commuting, the most critical of the actual driving skills is merging.  Make sure you know how to merge.  Practice the merging skills described here for all merges.  Make them become your habit.  Everything will flow more smoothly when you are good at merging.

On freeways, the lane adjacent to the middle divider, lane 1, has the right-of-way over the vehicles to their right when the lane 1 vehicle's rear bumper is in front of the vehicle in lane 2.  This allows the drivers in the left lanes to exit the roadway.  In this case, the lane 2 driver is required to allow the lane 1 vehicle to merge.  Subsequently, the motorist in lane 3 has the right of way over the vehicle in lane 4, if he is in front of him.  To have the right of way, they need to be safely past the adjacent vehicles front bumper.  When a driver ahead of you, in the adjacent lane on the left, looks like they want to merge, remember they have the right of way, so allow them to merge.  Don't expect the same consideration from the other drivers when you go to merge.  If a car in the lane to your right thinks you may want to merge (cut them off), they will almost always close the gap on the vehicle in front of them making it impossible to merge.  Follow the instructions below to prevent this from occurring.

Merging is also required whenever you don't have the clear right of way.  For a two-way street, it's usually a simple matter of waiting until there is a large enough gap for you to enter the roadway without impeding any traffic.  Merging onto a freeway or merging to change lanes requires small at-speed adjustments to make a smooth merge.

Keep an eye on the other motorists.  Drivers often betray their lane changing intentions unconsciously by gently swerving toward the lane dividing line when they intensely check their side rearview mirror in preparation for their merge.  Allow them to merge.  Often, immediately merging into the vacancy they created by their merge will allow you to advance through traffic.

On some expressway access ramps, traffic exiting and entering must completely cross.  This is essentially just an exchange of lanes.  Motorists traveling through these interchanges on a regular basis will maintain a good speed, aligning in a proper zipper fashion between the vehicles wanting to cross, and then smoothly merge.  Motorists unfamiliar with these interchanges tend to block merging vehicles, because they are afraid of getting trapped.  This slows traffic in both lanes significantly.  Do not drive side-by-side with another vehicle on one of these ramps or you may be forced to exit or slow excessively.  As you approach the ramp, size up the crossing vehicles to determine your merge slot, move to your slot, and merge smoothly.

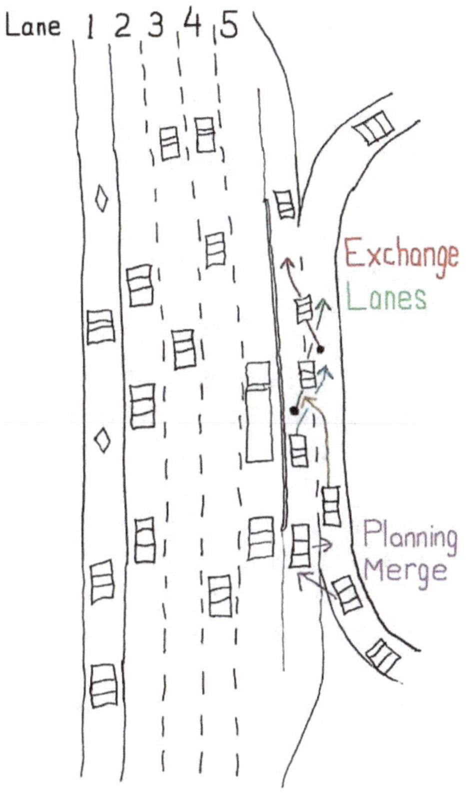


Exchanging Lanes

In most places, it is common practice for motorists to allow cars to smoothly merge like a zipper, every other car from each merging lane merges into one lane.  This is efficient.  Allow others to merge in front of you using this method.  You are required to allow only one vehicle to merge and it is discourteous to the people behind you to allow more than one vehicle to merge in front of you.

**The Merge**
- Maneuver to a gap in the adjacent lane.
- Match the lane speed of the neighboring lane.  Don't tap your brakes or otherwise impede your lane.
- Signal directly before you start your move and then merge smoothly, accelerating slightly to prevent jamming the trailing vehicles.
- If necessary or advantageous, change two lanes.  This can help you advance through traffic and will reduce any driver anger related to the merge.  Either way, make sure you don't tap your brakes, and focus on the new car now in front of you.

**Merge Factors**
- Don't hesitate; if you do, the trailing vehicle in the neighboring lane will probably move quickly forward to prevent your merge.
- Merging with confidence will subconsciously cause the motorists in adjacent lanes to slow a little bit.  This allows for an even easier merge.
- Don't use your brakes when changing lanes.  Your goal is to cause no one to brake in any lane because of your merge.
- You can't merge when you're not moving.  If your lane is stopped and an adjacent lane continues to move more than 5 mph faster than your lane, a merge will likely interrupt the traffic flow in both lanes.

- You can't merge into a lane that is stopped.  Many people, who haven't learned how to merge, stop in-lane so they can merge into a stopped lane.  This behavior causes catastrophic cascade braking, slowing vehicles and inhibiting the flow of traffic.  Do not participate in this behavior.
- In times of decreased visibility, such as during twilight, merge 10% into the desired lane to ensure the other motorists see you, then complete the merge.
- Be aware of the driver profiles of the motorists in the merge lane.  Certain profiles drive erratically and are difficult to follow.

**Reasons for Improper Merges**
- Poor visibility
- Going too slow to merge
- Not looking
- Panic
- Missed exit/turn

**Results**

Cascading braking in both lanes.  Often spreading to other lanes because drivers behind only see the spreading brake lights.

There is no excuse for an improper merge.  If you can't merge effectively, you don't merge.  If you missed your turn, you go around – however long that will take.  **Don't risk vehicle damage or people's lives because you missed a turn.**


## Accordion Opportunities

In multi-lane traffic, after a traffic light or other bottleneck, when the traffic starts to move, gaps appear as the drivers allow for their standard start gap.  This is called the traffic accordion.  This is the best time to merge into an adjacent lane.  You can often advance a great distance relative to the rest of the traffic by using the diagonal maneuver – see below.

Look for lanes with big gaps between vehicles.  These will often compress, and huge gains can be made against the adjacent lanes.  Beware though, the lane probably had big gaps because one or more of the drivers are driving slowly, so once the lane has fully compressed, prepare to change lanes after the traffic accordion opens.  (See the "Merging" section under *Driving Skills* for more information.)

Be observant on your commute.  Traffic accordions occur frequently.  This is one of the most reliable traffic patterns that you can use to your advantage.  Don't force it, learn the patterns of your traffic.

Also, be thankful for predictably slow drivers.  They will block traffic, creating mini-accordions.  You can advance by merging in front of them.

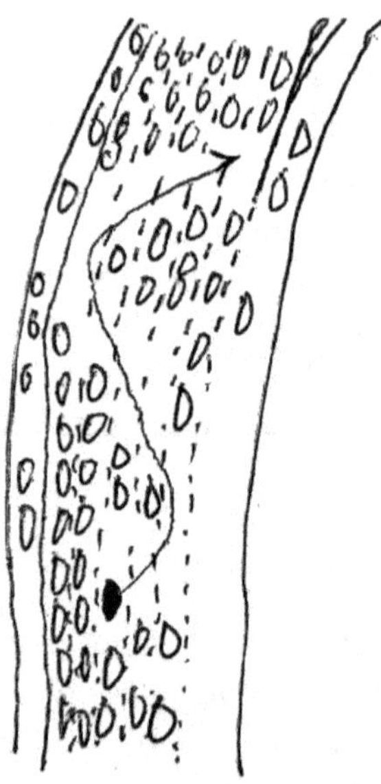

Diagonal maneuver, taking advantage of a traffic accordion

A major traffic advancement can be made due to lane compression during a traffic accordion.  When you sense that the traffic is condensing, join the "truck lanes" and advance against the adjoining lanes.  The number of trucks is much lower than the number of other vehicles in the "commuter lanes," so when they condense, they condense significantly more than the other lanes.  As mentioned above, each vehicle will wait for the vehicle in front of them to start moving, usually about 2 seconds, before moving themselves.  This is the standard start gap.  The trucks may wait 3 or 4 seconds, but they will still maintain a significant advancement.  Merge to the left as the traffic opens.

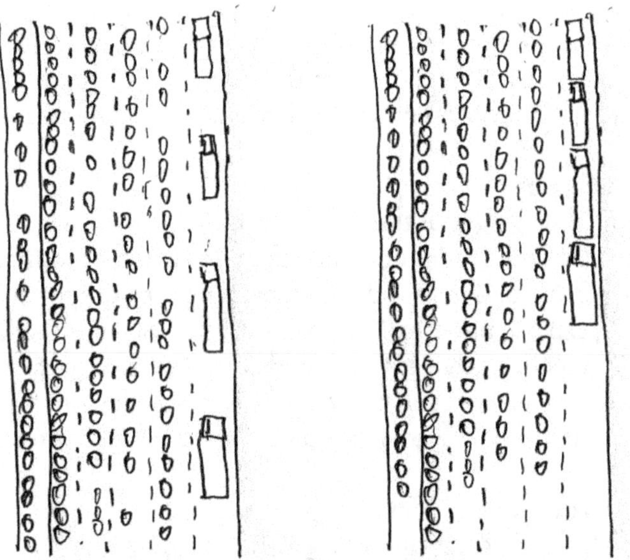

Accordion Truck Lanes – the trucks compress significantly more

## Lane Management

I've heard many people say, "I always seem to choose the slowest lane." That feeling is caused by their general lack of observation during the commute. Most drivers rarely notice the other lanes until theirs isn't moving. They may have been slowly passing vehicles for some time, but until they slow, they won't notice the other lanes. There is a general back and forth between the lanes as drivers ahead merge in slow traffic. Observation of the patterns will help you select the lanes most likely to regularly advance for a particular section of the roadway.

### Close the Gap

At all times, close the gap with the vehicle in front of you. Close to your usual trailing gap. If you change lanes and a large gap is now available, close it. A whole world of passing opportunities will appear. On your commute keep track of changes in the roadway. This will define your usual lane management.

### Lane Selection

- At lights go for the shortest lane.
- On your commute notice temporary right lanes that exist for a mile and then force a right exit or merge. Explore the use of these lanes, they will usually allow you to easily pass large numbers of cars. Occasionally, you may get stuck and lose a little time, but in the long run, you'll save a lot of time. I get stuck about once a month.
- Look for add-on lanes.
- Keep track of lane endings that force mergers.
- Track regular locations where large numbers of vehicles exit your commuting route. Large numbers of motorists turning left or right will first clog the through lane, but as they merge into the turn lanes, the through lane becomes unclogged – usually right at the turn. Watch

for these on your regular commute and plan to merge into these lanes as the motorists vacate.  Watch for non-turning slow vehicles that are slow to close the gap (most frequently occurring in the right lane) on the vehicle in front of them.  You may need to merge away from them before the other traffic closes.

**Construction or Accident Bottlenecks**

It's usually best to stay in the lane that will end.  Most people don't want to get stuck and will merge early.  They are nervous about aggravating some driver further up, who has been patiently waiting their turn.  The fact is, that most people slow excessively for these events, perhaps because the unexpected on their usual commute snaps them into a state of interest.  Don't confuse this with active traffic concentration.  In any case, their early merge usually allows you to pass dozens if not hundreds of vehicles.  Typically, once you are near the end of the closing lane, there are plenty of opportunities to easily merge without contributing to the congestion.  By the way, from a scientific perspective, the traffic will move faster if all of the lanes are used for as long as possible.  The counterproductive, congestion-enhancing activity of an early merge is driven by sight.  For example, if a normal three lane road narrows at some point to two, a person using the merge early philosophy might as well merge as soon as they enter the roadway; even if the bottleneck is three miles away.  Where does this person draw the merge line?  Usually it's about a quarter of a mile (400m) from the bottleneck.  It must have something to do with the fact they can clearly now see it.

## Advancing Through Traffic

The primary goal of this tome is to help you advance through traffic.  Using the information you've learned about the psychology of drivers and driving environments, and using the driving skills you've improved, you are already working your way through traffic faster.  In this section, a variety of additional techniques are described, which will allow you to advance further and more quickly.

**Freeway Off Ramps**
As traffic merges into the freeway exit lane, space opens in the right lanes.  Merge to the right lanes as they advance.  Then as soon as you pass the exit, quickly merge left across all lanes before the on-ramp traffic has a chance to stall the right lanes.  Nearly all drivers avoid this maneuver, but it will advance you though traffic in a predictable pattern on a daily basis.

Remember the lanes are all moving at different speeds.  What appears to be a static formation in the illustration, is actually a perpetuating pattern in the traffic.  It's very similar to ripple pattens in moving water.  If you watch the traffic at various locations for long enough, you'll notice distinctive patterns emerging regularly in the way the traffic moves.

Diagonally alternate between right and left lanes.  Move to the right lanes for exit ramps.  The exiting vehicles will allow the traffic in the right lanes to move more quickly.  Then immediately move left to avoid the congestion generated by the vehicles joining the freeway from the on-ramp.  An on-ramp that is an add-on lane will generate only moderately more congestion, so keep track of how the traffic behaves at these locations and define a strategy that will work consistently for you.

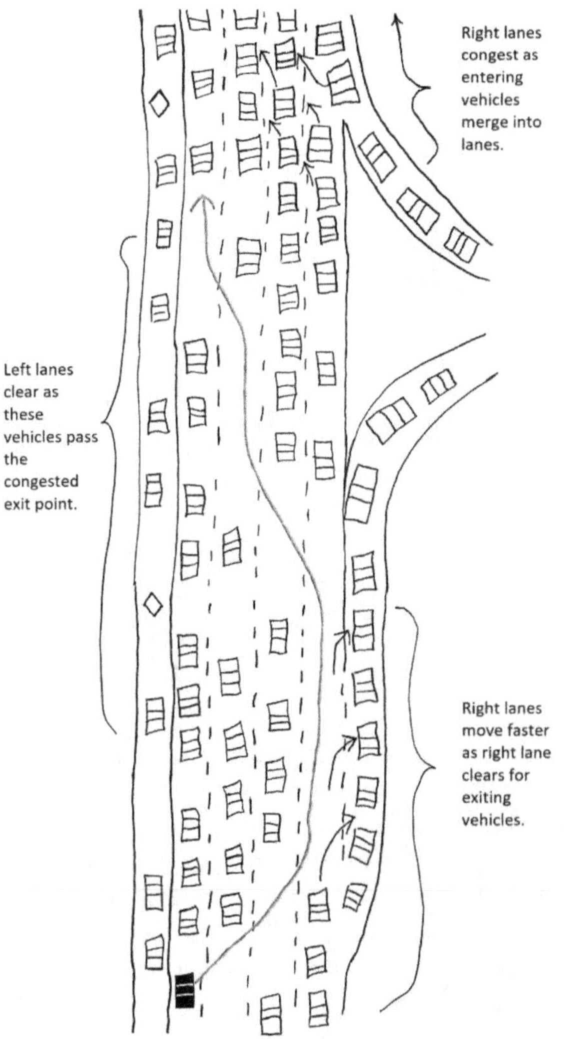



Diagonal Maneuver at Off-Ramp

Another exit ramp strategy is to take advantage of long, empty freeway exit ramps.  If your commute takes you past one of these, you can use them to advance around some vehicles.  Join the exit ramp, pass a number of cars and then merge back in to the flow of traffic.

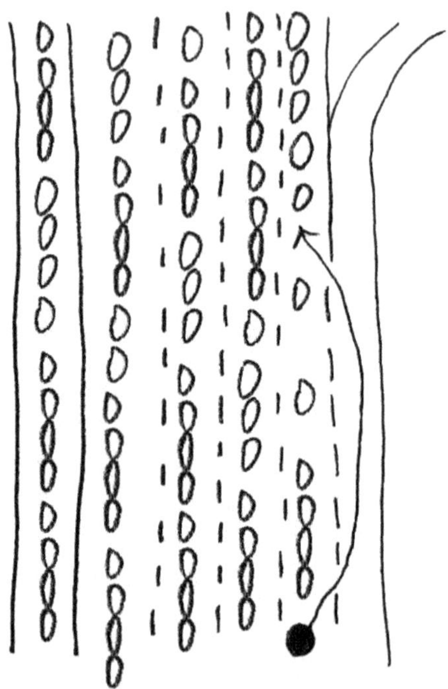

Vacant long freeway exit lane

## Freeway Frontage Lanes

Many freeways have full frontage roads that parallel the freeway.  Examine these for opportunities where you can advance past stalled freeway traffic.  The in-lane freeway traffic won't know you've just passed them, they'll think you're just now joining the freeway.

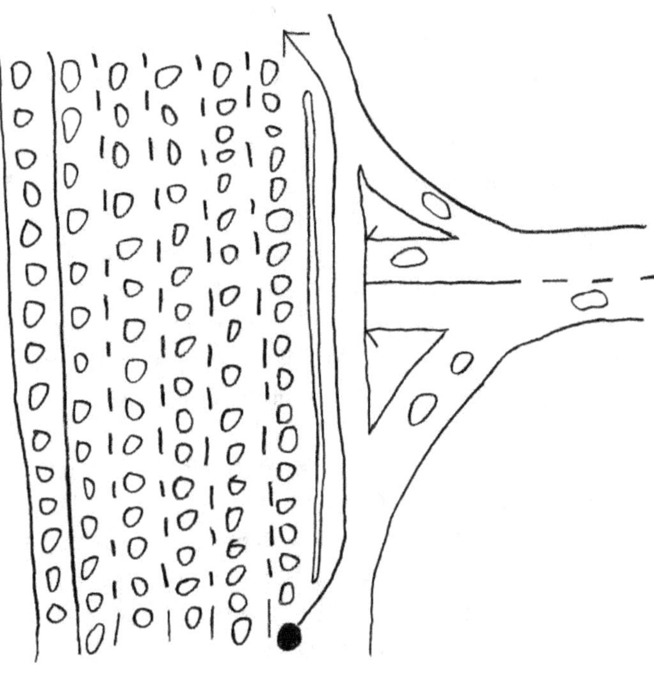

Freeway frontage lanes

## Merge to the Right Paradox

If all drivers would move to right after passing, the roads could
be narrower all across the country.  In some foreign countries,
drivers are trained to merge to the right after passing.  This is
the law in most every state in America, but it is rarely enforced.
Most drivers usually stay left after passing.  Perhaps because
municipalities had a fairly easy time gaining needed rights of
way for expanding roadways, little effort has been made to
enforce merge-to-the-right-after-passing laws in America.

Everyone has always been told that the left lane is the "fast
lane" and is for the fast drivers.  When we're learning to drive,
we hear, "Don't get in the left lane on the freeway unless you
want to go really fast.  Some of those drivers in the left lane are

very fast and aggressive." At certain times it's true, but most every day, the left lanes get clogged with everyone wanting to go fast, so, the traffic in the left lanes go slower and slower. Everyone has also been told that the right lane is the "slow lane." And now everyone believes that the right lanes are the truck lanes or slow lanes.

What this means is that the **right lanes are almost always the faster lanes**. Keep your eyes on certain trucks and vehicles in each lane. Then in a mile, compare the relative distances to each of these same vehicles. You'll find that as the traffic increases, the right lanes tend to move the fastest.

Dr. Kerner, referenced earlier, stated that internationally on freeways, the right lane (left lane if you drive on the left) tends to move the slowest. This is true when you measure on a macro level and on long-term averages, but when you are in the traffic, you have an opportunity to avoid known bottlenecks. Occasionally, you need to merge to the left lanes to avoid the congestion created by one of these perturbances. Traffic is dynamic and will change. Being observant of the traffic patterns as they evolve will allow you to advance through the congestion effectively.


**Traffic Light Advice**
Navigating a regular commute nearly always includes at least a few traffic lights. I had one commute where I had over 70 traffic lights each way. It's very beneficial to take advantage of traffic patterns around the traffic lights.

- Count the number of cars in each lane and always go for the shortest lane. (Unless you have specific prior knowledge that the lane will become congested shortly after the light.) Often you can't see all of the vehicles directly, so count the shadows they leave on the road.

- If you have three lanes headed your way and all of the lanes have the same number of vehicles, always go for the middle lane; unless of course, one of the vehicles is in the questionable category. (In the "Driver Profiles" section, see profiles marked with an asterisk *.)
- The size of the vehicle is less important than the number.
- Count old, poorly maintained vehicles as 1.5 or 2 depending on how poorly maintained the vehicle appears.
- Most new commercial trucks and buses accelerate quickly, and buses may move right to stop immediately after the light leaving a large opening in the lane if they merge completely out of the traffic lanes.
- Count motorcyclists carefully. Most will accelerate quickly off the line, but a few will start quickly and then stall in speed. Count them at the light at .5 or less.
- Don't wait for your standard start gap, start moving as soon as the vehicle in front of starts moving. Adjust your trailing gap as the vehicle accelerates.
- Those who drive like this book describes, should be counted as zero. They will get out of the way when being passed. And because they are paying attention, they will be ready to move once the light changes.

**Lane Compressions**
Time your lane changes to take advantage of lane compressions at lights and construction sites.


**Leave yourself options**
In lanes, always look for an out. Heavy traffic increases your need for alternate routes or extra lane passes (see the next section). Being in traffic increases your need for an out. Be able to avoid accidents by having an out. An 'out' is an alternate direction you can steer to avoid a collision. Also, plan to have

alternate routes – they are useful when there's an accident or major roadway obstruction.

**Extra Lanes**
It has been proven mathematically, through queue theory models, that you should always use extra lanes when available. You are not being rude by passing hundreds of cars, you are being efficient.  You are not slowing the adjacent traffic, so don't feel guilty.

Extra lane ends after traffic signal

Extra lane ending with forced exit

**Leader of the Pack**

As discussed in the section, *The Psychology of Drivers*, drivers who feel like they are the one advancing through traffic will often drive much more observantly than they typically might. They become the leader of the pack.  Encourage this reaction in other drivers by merging behind them when they make a move. Don't get too close; if they feel you tailgating, it will have the opposite effect.  Drivers tend to speed up when you merge behind them.  If you make them feel like they are now the leader of the pack, they will subconsciously accelerate and attempt to advance through traffic.

**False Sense of Slowing**

If there's a large gap between the driver in front of you and the vehicle in front of them, you can try the false sense of slowing ruse to get them to close the gap.  Encourage them to drive a little faster by lagging back then moving up.  They will instinctively think they're the one slowing down and will speed up a bit, if they have room.  Watch their rearview mirror, when they aren't looking at you, close your gap a bit.  When they look at you, release the throttle, coasting back a little.  They'll get the feeling that they're driving too slow and will usually speed up.  Tailgating will make them slow down, so don't.

Create a false sense of slowing in a lagging driver ahead of you

## Exiting a Freeway

Observe the freeway exit patterns on your usual commute.  During rush hour, most people pile into the exit lane half a mile or more from their exit.  They are afraid of having to force a merge.  The exit line will accordion multiple times over this distance.  Practice first by jumping to the first open accordion space, so you can "short the line."  Once you feel comfortable with this go all of the way to the solid white line before merging into the exit lane.  You may eliminate several light cycles on the exit ramp.

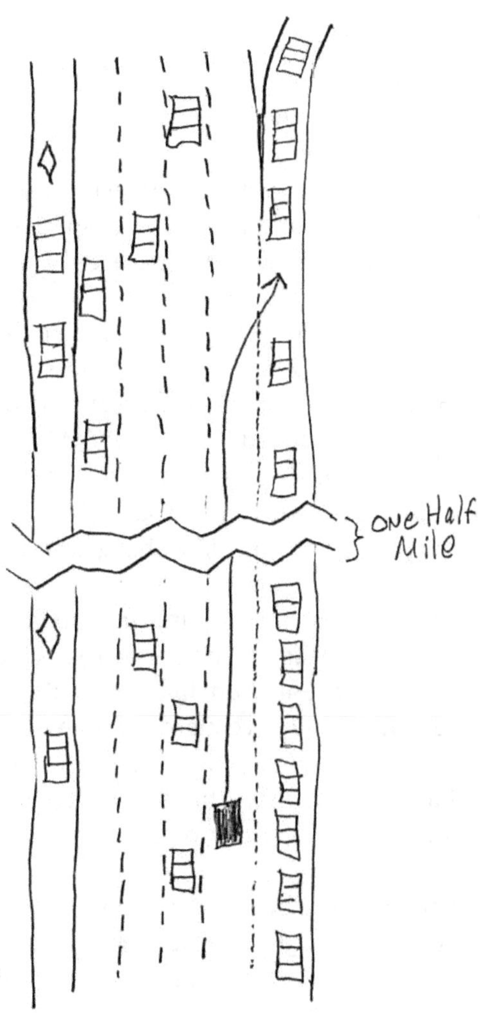


Exiting a Freeway – long exit line

## Traffic Lights

Scan the traffic signals as far down the road as you can see. Note the daily patterns.  If a light is going stale (has been green for a long time) review the traffic density ahead and determine which lane is most likely to be the shortest at the light.  As you get closer to the traffic signal, count the number of cars in each lane and always go for the shortest lane.  Unless you've observed otherwise, play the odds at traffic lights.  Select the lane with the shortest line, even if the lane has a truck in it; it will likely move faster off the line than the lanes with more vehicles.  Take into consideration any prior specific knowledge you have that the lane will become congested after the light. Often you can't see all of the vehicles directly, so count the shadows they leave on the road.  Remember, at traffic lights, motorcycles count for about .5 cars, maybe less.  They accelerate very rapidly due to the low weight to power ratio. They might not hit a top speed you'd like, so it is usually wise to switch to another lane once you've moved off the line.  If all of the lanes are equal, go for the middle lane.  That will give you more merging options once the light changes green.

The time left on the crosswalk sign is a great indicator of how stale a traffic light has become.  If you see the 'white walking guy' or if the seconds countdown on the pedestrian crossing is greater than 5, you should have plenty of time to make the light.  If the pedestrian crossing signal starts flashing or if the flashing red hand goes to a solid hand, you've got about three seconds before the light changes to yellow.

When you come to a stop behind a vehicle at a traffic light, you should usually leave enough room so you can see their tires. This should be your standard stopping gap.  It's probably a little more distance from the car in front of you than you usually use, but it will give you better visibility and will leave you enough room for an out.  If the vehicle in front of you stalls or hits the car in front of them, you will still be able to get around them needing to put your car in reverse.

When making a left turn on a surface street, try to keep your speed up as you approach the left turn.  Try to time your left turn through traffic at speed, to prevent an unnecessary stop.  Look carefully at the crosswalk and the sidewalks to make sure you have a clear path.  This applies to both traffic lights and mid-block left turns.

If a turn bay on your usual commute is often so full that it extends into the through lanes, move closer to the vehicle in front of you than your usual stopping gap.  If each vehicle in the turn lane does the same, more vehicles will be able to move all of the way into the turning bay and will allow through traffic to continue unimpeded.

If a light is going stale or if it's red, remove your foot from the accelerator and coast toward the light.  If someone wants to make a quick merge in front of you, let them.  In most cases these drivers will move quickly off the line.  Also, it can be a rough ride when you're accelerating toward stopped cars and then need to slam on the brakes to stop.  This not only creates a rough ride, but it is also tough on the brakes, fuel consumption, and tire wear, and can result in someone rear-ending you.

If you planned on proceeding through an intersection and the light turns red on you, consider one of your planned alternate routes.  If you can quickly make a right turn that will take you to one of your alternate routes, you may be able to save time.  If the intersection has long red lights, a two minute longer detour will save time if the light cycle is five minutes.  Never take an unvetted alternate route, especially if you're in a hurry!

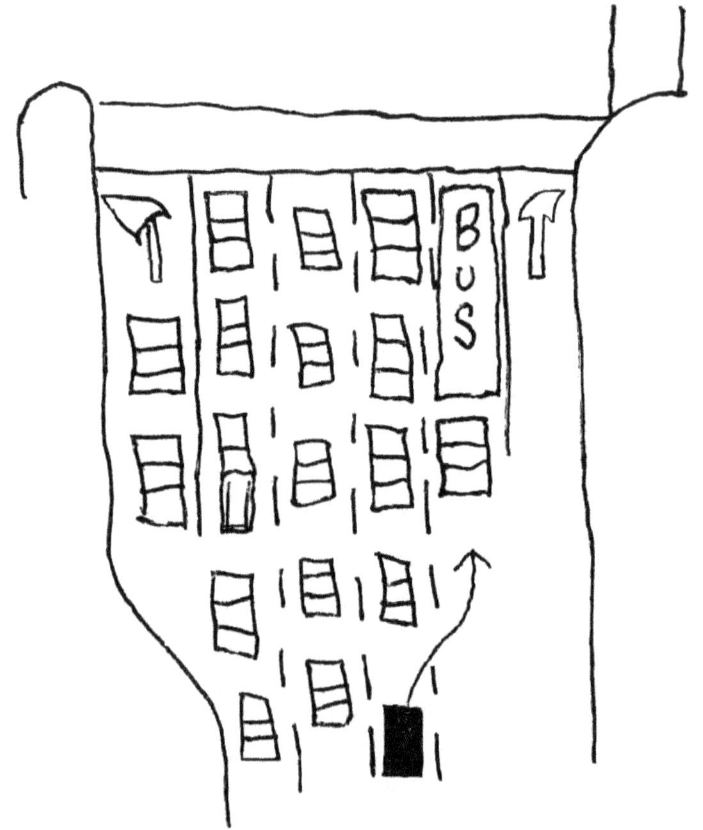

Selecting the shortest lane.

At intersections with left-turn arrows, you can often make quick right-turns when the light is red for you, but the cross traffic has its protected left-turn signals active.  Be mindful of motorists attempting to make a U-turn on the protected arrow.  Other than the occasional U-turner, your turn is protected from oncoming traffic by the drivers turning left.

If you need to turn right just past a traffic light, perhaps you need to enter a retail business parking lot, you should delay your merge into the right lane until after you've moved through

the intersection.  This is especially true if there isn't a separate
right-turn lane.  Many motorists turning right off of the main
road will slow significantly or even stop completely to survey
the intersection before completing their turn.  Many will do this
even if they have the clear right of way.  In addition, crossing
pedestrians are common in urban areas and the lane may stall
for more than a minute waiting for the pedestrians to clear the
crosswalk.  This could cause you to miss the light.  Some light
cycles are more than five minutes, so it could be a long wait.

## Weather

Know your driving skill level for different weather conditions.
Driving on icy roads is extremely hazardous even for
experienced drivers and should be avoided when possible.
There are occasions when the weather conditions change
dramatically while you're at work and then, at the end of the
day, you've got a full-blown blizzard in progress.  To make sure
your commute is as safe as possible, work on your extreme
weather driving skills when you have the opportunity in a safe
environment.  For example, an empty parking lot is a good place
to practice driving on ice.

Flooding presents very different challenges.  Unless you know
for certain that you can cross a low water crossing, don't make
the attempt.  If you do decide to make the attempt, don't cross
slowly.  That is the best way to drown the engine.  Unless the
water is uniformly shallow, make sure you have enough speed
to cross the entire flooded area.  If the engine does stall, at least
you're not in the middle of the low-water crossing.  That is a
very bad place to be, especially if the water continues to rise.  A
number of states have stupid motorist laws that will fine you for
the inconvenience of having to rescue you.  Add the fine to the
cost of having your vehicle towed out of the low-water crossing

and the cost of vehicle repairs and it will be extremely expensive.

During a flash flood of the Pantano Wash in Tucson, I saw a couple of people attempt to cross the 200 yards of quickly moving relatively shallow water.  Several had water washing over their hoods and had stalled.  A man on a tractor came to their rescue, pulling them to safety.  The fellow on the tractor then decided to attempt a crossing.  I guess he figured that he had plenty of clearance to make the crossing without any fear of stalling his tractor.  He proceeded quickly to the midpoint where the water was about three feet deep.  Suddenly, the large rear tires floated off of the road and the whole tractor moved about eight feet sideways and tilted 45 degrees wrenching the driver from his seat.  He was clinging to the steering wheel, his legs dangling in the torrential water flow.  He was able to pull himself up onto the high side of the tractor.  He was standing precariously on the tractor as waves of rising water rocked the tractor, threatening to roll it completely over. He looked at us hoping we could rescue him, but there was no way anyone watching could help him.  Luckily for him, the waters didn't continue to rise and then slowly began to recede. He was eventually rescued by the Sheriff's rescue team.  This fellow was certain he could cross the low water crossing, but obviously couldn't.

Driving in extremely hot conditions can cause many problems as well.  Extreme heat can be very hard on your vehicle.  Ensure you're maintaining your vehicle for your specific driving environments.  Make sure you carry plenty of extra water in stainless steel containers.  Stainless steel won't release hazardous chemicals into the water when heated – especially useful in the hottest parts of the country.

# Passing

Passing is not the same as merging.  On a large multi-lane road, you can pass (overtake) a car in a neighboring lane and never merge in front of them.  For the purposes of commuting, passing is the act of moving past another vehicle on two-way, two-lane roadway.  These roads have one lane on each side separated by a dashed yellow line.

Passing is the driving skill that's most stressful for drivers.  Most people will not attempt a pass unless they can see well down the road and do not see any oncoming traffic.  Fearfulness or over-hesitation can cause huge jams on these roads especially when there's an especially slow vehicle and the car directly behind refuses to pass.

Become a **passing surgeon**.  Practice every time you can. Observe how far away each vehicle appears as they approach. Count how many seconds it takes distant approaching vehicles to pass by you.  Then count how many seconds it takes for you to complete different types of passes at various speeds.  Write it down.

For me, on a highway where I'm going to pass a vehicle going 50 mph, it takes me six seconds to pass a passenger vehicle and nine seconds to pass a bus or semi-tractor trailer.  These are prepared passes where I stand off from the vehicle to be passed and then as the last approaching vehicle nears, I accelerate in-lane toward the vehicle to be passed.  By the time the approaching vehicle passes, I am already at passing speed and I can execute a precision pass.

One time, I was on a remote, moderately curvy highway in rural Arizona and I came upon 40 vehicles stacked up behind one very slow driver.  Behind the very slow vehicle were four drivers who were afraid to pass.  If the drivers immediately behind the slow vehicle would have passed, everyone would have been able to eventually pass.  In this case, there were too many drivers directly behind the slow vehicle who were unwilling to look for passing opportunities.  This created a half-mile long chain of cars moving 25 mph below the speed limit.  Many of these drivers were angry and frustrated.  Certainly, the driver at the front should have pulled off to let everyone pass, but they did not.  Over a period of about half an hour I was able to pass my way up the line of vehicles, a little at a time, until I got to the group of four.  They were all bumper-to-bumper and didn't want to let anyone to pass them.  They wanted everyone to suffer as they were.  I backed off a little and waited for a good passing opportunity and passed all five vehicles in one pass.  There was very little oncoming traffic in this remote area, so there was plenty of time to pass.  I supposed that the four reluctant passers were waiting for a passing lane.  There wasn't one.

Two-lane passing

## Traffic Circles

Whether one of these is on your regular commute or not, learn how to efficiently merge into the traffic circle and continue to your exit.

For people driving on the right, the basic rules are:
1.  Circulate counterclockwise.
2.  Yield to the vehicles on your left.

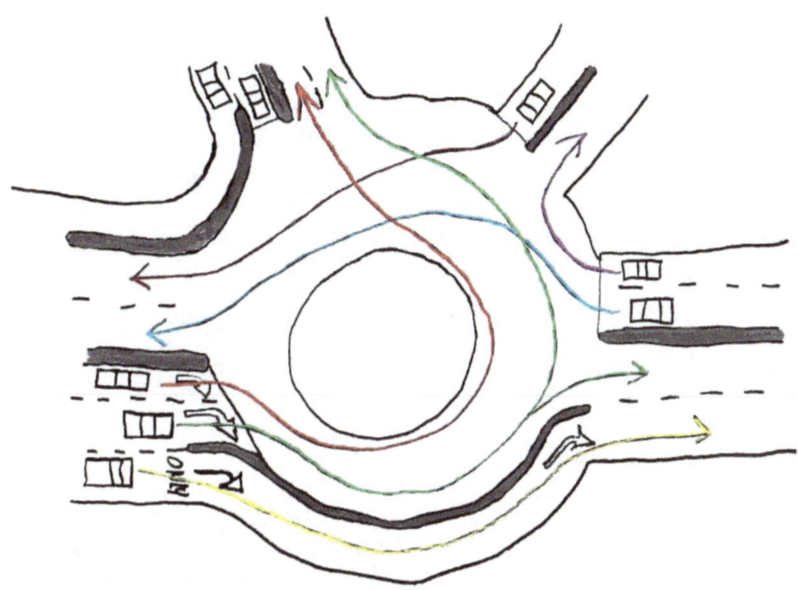


Navigating a traffic circle

The traffic already in the circle has the right of way over those entering.  As you approach the circle, plan your entrance.  Use the available signage and lane markings to choose the optimal entrance path.  Know which exit is yours before you enter the circle.  Try not to stop before entering.  Merge in smoothly.  On large multi-lane traffic circles, where your exit is one of the last ones, merge toward the center of the circle so you're not forced off before your exit.  If your exit has multiple exit lanes, use one of the left lanes to advance against the right lanes.  (See the red route in the illustration.)

Watch for the unexpected.  Cyclists or pedestrians often don't have any traffic signals to assist them, so sometimes you'll have a pedestrian dash out in an attempt to cross.  Make an effort not to crowd cyclists.  It's hard enough to ride a bicycle in traffic, let alone around a traffic circle.

After I graduated from college, I rode a bicycle across Europe.  I spent a couple of months riding across continental Europe before taking a train to London.  My departure back to the States was from Heathrow Airport.  I had to ride my bike 18 miles through London to the airport.  There were so many roundabouts (traffic circles), all going the wrong way, that I thought I was going to die in one of them.  Fortunately, the drivers were used to seeing cyclists and they all avoided me.  Please be as courteous to the cyclists you encounter as the London drivers were to me.

## Freeway - Rural

You may have observed remote area traffic pulses – often in extremely remote areas.  A group of vehicles – sometimes 50 or more – will be trapped together.  Usually everyone lines up in the left lane, hoping to eventually pass.  I've seen vehicles lined up for more than quarter of a mile.  This is usually caused by a slow vehicle passing a slightly slower vehicle.  I've observed a pass of this type taking 25 minutes – more than 20 miles.  Meanwhile, other normally faster traffic is stalled and a clog occurs.  This also happens in cities, but is much harder to detect because there are generally more vehicles and numerous on- and off-ramps.  How to deal with this?

Timing:

- Pass on the right – they won't want you to (you should stand in line).  I've passed more than 40 cars in one pass like this.
- Use your merge skills to merge to the left when you approach the slow vehicle.  Make sure you maintain your speed as you approach the end of the left-lane clog.  These drivers won't have seen you yet, so you can smoothly merge into one of their accordion gaps.  Keep practicing.
- Move right again as soon as your pass is complete.  Everyone should be in the right lane unless   passing.

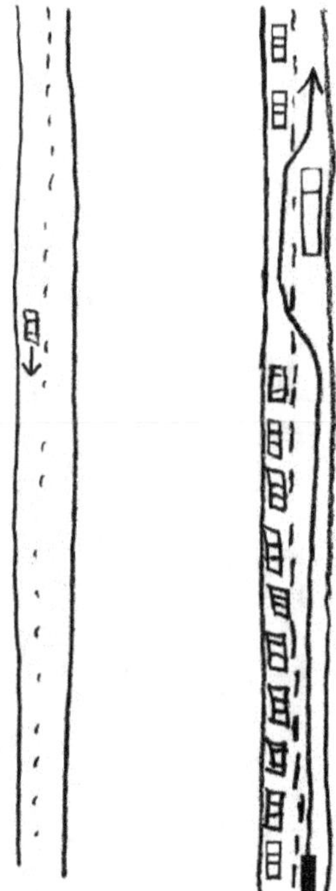

Rural freeway with long lines in left lane

## Exit Strategy

Avoid angry or erratic drivers.  The vast majority of time, a driver's anger will be rooted elsewhere and has nothing to do with you.  They had a bad day; perhaps his wife ran off with a rock musician or the IRS has announced a complete audit.  In all cases, don't get sucked in to their anger.  Erratic drivers can be perplexing and sometimes entertaining, but they are dangerous.  Try to advance away from them.

Sometimes it's wise to completely get away from an erratic motorist.  At a point when they're in front of you, take an exit when it becomes inconvenient for them to exit at the same time.  Don't telegraph your intentions.  This works well on a freeway.  If you think you're being followed, don't drive home or to work, drive to the nearest police or fire station.

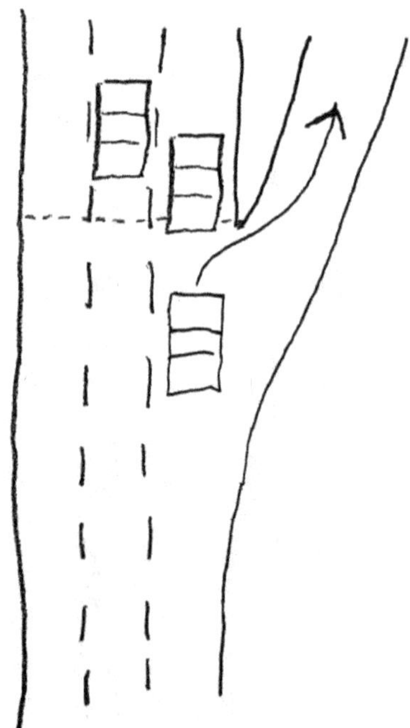

Exit strategy – the erratic driver is past the dotted line

# Commuting by Bicycle

When I was in college, I commuted ten miles each way to campus through heavy traffic for two years training for my European bicycle tour.  I covered the distance through traffic in 27 minutes.  That was from my front door to my seat in class.  After graduation, I rode a bicycle from Rome to Spain and other European locations.  I've been hit about six times.  Only once did I need to go to the hospital; the other times were either at a slow speed or I was bounced off of the road where I was able to recover control.

### Bicycle Safety in Traffic

As a cyclist you want to be easily visible and very predictable.  Traffic can overtake you quickly so clearly signal your intentions.  If you have to stop, get off the road.  Know the laws and how laws apply differently to bicycles.   Wear a helmet!

### Expediting the Ride

- Draft when you can.  Any object moving through air creates a slipstream on the side opposite the direction of motion.  The slipstream is comprised of air moving with the object and is referred to as the draft.  The larger the object, the larger the draft of air behind it.  Cyclists often draft behind each other in lines.  They switch lead cyclist in a rotating fashion.  When drafting, it feels like the wind is always at your back.  It significantly reduces the effort required to maintain speed.  Buses pull a lot of air in their draft and new models are very clean, so they can make an excellent draft choice, but be aware that in some locations you can be cited for tailgating.
- At lights, you can often lean lightly against pickup trucks or similar vehicle where you don't need to touch their

paint.  I usually aim for something made from chrome.  This allows you to keep your toes in the toe clips.  When the light changes, you can much more easily get moving again.

- If possible, select a route that has bike lanes, especially when going uphill.
- Use bike lanes downhill or in flat areas if the surface is smooth.  Often the bike lanes have not been maintained and can become very rough.  If that's the case, I usually ride on the road with traffic.

One of my commuting bicycles

# *Responsibilities*

You have numerous responsibilities while driving.  The reason you're required to have auto insurance is that a lot of people are irresponsible.  You've studied the psychology of driving, reviewed the different environments presented to motorists, practiced the driving skills and now you need to make sure you use your knowledge responsibly.

Know your local traffic laws.  Use this knowledge to contribute to the free flow of traffic.

## Eliminate Bad Habits

From time to time everyone will be guilty of some driving bad habit.  Identify when you fall into the trap of one and work to break the habit.

**Some Driving Sins:**
Staying left after passing
Trying to merge when moving too slowly
Trying to merge into a lane that is stopped
Lane drifting
Riding your brakes – red tail lights slows all of the drivers behind you
Using emergency lanes
Preventing others from passing
Rubbernecking
Driving erratically
Driving on autopilot
Using both feet in a vehicle with an automatic transmission
Honking when angry – most people who honk are angry, honk only to alert another motorist

See the prior sections to learn how to eliminate these and other bad habits.

## Your Vehicle

Maintain your vehicle.  Don't just put fuel in it, change the oil regularly.  Check your tire pressure and check the tread for wear.  Keep your car clean.  Make sure your mirrors, wipers, brake lights and turn signals are working properly.  Follow your owner's manual for other regular maintenance.  If you don't have the owner's manual, you can probably download it from the manufacturer's website.

Understand the capabilities of your vehicle in your commute.  Commuting is not a race; it's a pattern of movement.  You don't need the most powerful vehicle; you just need something that works well.   Know the dimensions of your vehicle and make sure you know the clearances on all corners.

For more information vehicles, refer to the information on Vehicle Operation in the Driving Skills section.


## Pay Attention

Driving is dangerous.  Make sure you constantly survey what's up ahead and what may be coming up from behind.  Don't look at passengers or your phone.  Your primary responsibility is to successfully move your vehicle from one place to another without causing any damage to anything.  This can't be accomplished when you're behind the wheel unless you commit to being observant and prepared.

It doesn't matter the location, the sunset, or the traffic accident on the shoulder of the road; you should never rubberneck or sightsee.  You are the driver; your responsibility is to get to your destination unscathed and that is difficult when you've rear-ended the car in front of you.  If you want to look, exit the roadway.

## Contribute to the Free Flow of Traffic

Most drivers are not engaged in the act of driving.  They are talking on their phones or thinking about work or other non-driving activities.  These drivers are on autopilot and have fallen into a herd mentality.  They will rubberneck, they will merge poorly, and they think little about driving and often impede the flow of traffic.  Do not be one of these drivers.  Be courteous; think about your actions.  Match the lane speed of the neighboring lane on a merge without impeding your lane and then execute your merge.  Always move right after you pass.  Remember, the less time you're on the road, the less congestion there is.

Maintain your stopping distance.  You should never have to slam on your brakes.  This makes for a rough ride and adversely affects all of the motorists behind you.

Allow others to pass you.  If other drivers appear observant and are working their way through traffic, allow them to merge in front of you.  In a worst-case scenario, you might lose eight seconds, but most passers continue to advance through traffic, opening passing opportunities for you too.
Let others pass:
-        If they're moving quickly, there's no need to block them.
-        Passers often open traffic in front of you and can potentially reduce your travel time.
-        Don't race – the other drivers may think they're racing you – let them pass.
-        Most people I pass don't realize I've passed them.

If the vehicle attempting to merge seems timid, perhaps by engaging their turn signal long before they start to merge, act fast.  It may seem rude, but these drivers will definitely slow your progress.  Either merge away immediately or try to encourage them to merge behind you.  Occasionally, these drivers attempt to merge right as their lane ends, nearly coming to a complete stop.  Try to avoid these situations by being observant.  At some point you're going you get stuck behind one of them; just be patient; you'll eventually advance away from them.

## Cascading Braking

Don't contribute to this.  It occurs when you tailgate, are inattentive or make a poor lane change.  Leave enough room between you and the driver in front of you, so that brake taps don't become brake slams.  I rarely need to use my brakes except at traffic lights.

## Lost or Disoriented

This occurs for everyone at some time.  If you recognize late that you're about to miss your exit or turn, do not cut across a lane of traffic to make this exit.  This is very dangerous and usually causes a cascading braking event in all of the lanes you traversed and possibly an accident.

Lost driver

# Don't Get Angry

Don't yell at the other drivers.  Many are not paying attention to what they are doing and are primarily concerned about themselves.  Many drivers are thinking about their day ahead or maybe the argument they had with their children this morning.

## Aggressive Driver Quiz

**Do You (check the boxes):**

| Y | N | | Y | N | |
|---|---|---|---|---|---|
| ☐ | ☐ | Use turn signals for both turns and lane changes. | ☐ | ☐ | Avoid taking more than one parking space. |
| ☐ | ☐ | Avoid hitting the vehicle parked next to you with your door. | ☐ | ☐ | Avoid parking in a space designated for the disabled. |
| ☐ | ☐ | Maintain appropriate following distance. | ☐ | ☐ | Use high beams only when necessary. |
| ☐ | ☐ | Yield to pedestrians. | ☐ | ☐ | Avoid blocking right turn lane. |
| ☐ | ☐ | Approach intersections and pedestrians at safe speeds. | ☐ | ☐ | Yield and move right for emergency vehicles. |
| ☐ | ☐ | Pass other vehicles on the left. | ☐ | ☐ | Rarely use your horn. |
| ☐ | ☐ | Avoid blocking passing lanes. | ☐ | ☐ | Refrain from flashing headlights. |
| ☐ | ☐ | Yield to faster vehicles by merging right. | ☐ | ☐ | Make careful and deliberate U-turns. |
| ☐ | ☐ | Use headlights in cloudy, rainy and low light conditions. | ☐ | ☐ | Maintain proper speeds around roadway crashes. |
| ☐ | ☐ | Provide appropriate distance when merging after passing a vehicle. | ☐ | ☐ | Avoid playing music loud enough for others to hear. |
| ☐ | ☐ | Keep right as much as possible. | ☐ | ☐ | Avoid driving when drowsy. |
| ☐ | ☐ | Make eye contact and signal intentions. | ☐ | ☐ | Avoid challenging other drivers. |
| ☐ | ☐ | Come to a safe stop at stop signs. | ☐ | ☐ | Ignore inappropriate gestures. |
| ☐ | ☐ | Stop for red traffic lights. | ☐ | ☐ | Get out of the way of aggressive drivers. |
| ☐ | ☐ | Follow right-of-way rules at four-way stops. | ☐ | ☐ | Maintain a speed appropriate for conditions. |
| ☐ | ☐ | Avoid using the phone while driving. | ☐ | ☐ | Avoid stopping in the road unnecessarily. |
| ☐ | ☐ | Drive at recommended speeds in construction zones. | ☐ | ☐ | Drive below the speed limit when conditions warrant. |
| ☐ | ☐ | Acknowledge intention of others. | ☐ | ☐ | Focus on driving and avoid distractions. |

**Score Yourself:**
**Count the Number of "No" Answers**

(1-3) Safe Driver      (4-7) Good Driver
(8-11) Semi-Aggressive Driver      (12+) Aggressive Driver

A good barometer.

## Carpooling

Carpool lanes are usually worthless during non-rush-hour times, but they are great for morning commutes.  If you're lucky enough to be in a carpool, that's great.  Still be aware that not all roads have carpool lanes and that often during afternoon commute hours, carpool lanes are slower than the right-most lane.  In the afternoon, a number of non-commuting drivers are still on the road and tend to be poor at merging.  They tend to get into the carpool lane and camp there.

Clogged carpool lane

## *Conclusions and Notes*

### Guarantee Reprised
If you've followed the advice in this publication and you still haven't seen a substantial reduction in your commuting time, then I have two more pieces of advice that might help:
- Don't commute during your local "rush hours."  Get up early or work late – whatever it takes to save your precious time.
- Work from home.  The commute from your bed to your home office is the best commute.

### Conclusions
Commuting is a necessity many of must deal with on a daily basis.  It is a grind on all of the commuters and it has real psychological and physiological effects on commuters.  By taking control of your commute you can reclaim lost hours each week for other more satisfying activities.

Remember to use the information in *The Psychology of Drivers* section to help you understand why the other motorists are behaving the way they are.  That will help reduce your stress during your regular commutes.  Understanding how this psychology is then impacted by driving environments will help you maintain composure when others become exasperated. Constantly work on refining your driving skills.  All of your driving experiences will improve.  It's easy to fall into bad habits, so remember your responsibilities when you're on the road.

**Notes**

**Tickets**

Occasionally you may be stopped by a patrol officer.  If so, consider this advice:

**At the Scene**

1. Turn off your vehicle and headlights.  Turn on your interior lights.  Remove hat and sunglasses.  Place hands at 10 and 2.  Don't get out.
2. Be courteous and respectful.
3. Be very polite.  Say nothing until he is finished speaking.
4. Once he has your information, ask him if you can speak to him about the violation.  If you broke the law and you know you won't take this to court, consider admitting it.  Tell him he was right to stop you.  Be sincere.  The better you make him feel the less likely he will be to cite you.
5. Ask to see radar.  Ask: When was the last time your radar was calibrated?  Where were you when you clocked my speed?  Were you moving? Be nice.
6. Plead your case.  Build rapport.  Try to stick to the truth and be sincere.

   **Stock answers for why you were speeding –** though excuses never worked for me
   a. You have to be moving at ___ speed to merge there
   b. Late for a funeral
   c. Need to pee
   d. Feel ill – coughing fit
   e. The music made me do it
   f. Take any excuse an officer provides – it's easier to convince someone what they already believe
   g. I was speeding, I'm sorry - ask for mercy
7. Do not create a scene or complain.  You don't want the officer to remember you.

Hopefully, that's enough for him to let you go with a stern warning.

**Got a Ticket?**
1.  Call the court clerk and ask if deferred adjudication is available.  In a number of locations, deferred adjudication eliminates the ticket as long as you don't get another ticket in the same jurisdiction again for a set number of days.  In some places it's 90 days and in others it's a year.  The fee is usually the full amount of the ticket plus court costs.  I've used this a number of times.
2.  Take driving school if you can.
3.  Plead your case to the judge and prosecutor before your court date and try to get the citation dismissed. Do not be a nuisance.
4.  Go to court.  Follow all court guidelines.  Make friends with the court clerk.  Use their name.
5.  Delay.
6.  Ask for alternate punishment.
7.  Understand your rights.
8.  Do not plead guilty.
9.  If found guilty appeal the verdict.  In most jurisdictions, an appeal is automatic, if you request one.

## *Exercises*

Practice these exercises to improve your skills.


### Exercise 1 - Observation

As you commute today, count the number of traffic lights on your route.  Then count how many made you come to a complete stop.  Do this for a couple of days and compare your results.


### Exercise 2 – Observation

On today's commute observe the different driver profiles and the different subconscious driving patterns.


### Exercise 3 – Planning

Take an alternate route today.  Make sure you track the commute time and make sure you have a little extra time in case the route is slower.


### Exercise 4 - Merging

Perfect your merging techniques.  Practice your merge timing and in-merge speed variations necessary to execute a smooth merge.

## Exercise 5 – Accordion Opportunities

You've been observing your commute's traffic patterns.  Use these patterns to identify some accordion opportunities and, if possible, execute a compete diagonal maneuver.

## Exercise 6 – Lane Management

As you commute through a section of traffic lights, select the shortest line.  See how your advancement compares to the other lanes.

## Exercise 7 – Advancing Through Traffic

Today, try to use a long freeway exit lane to advance around traffic or try to use a frontage road to bypass a section of traffic.

## Exercise 8 – Exiting a Freeway with a Long Exit Line

If your commute has jammed up traffic at your exit ramp, stay in a through lane until right before the exit.  Use your merging skills to slip in to the exit line as it does the traffic accordion.

## Exercise 9 – Passing

When you're on a two-lane roadway, count how many seconds distant vehicles take to get to you, so you can gauge how far the vehicles need to be for you to effectively pass.  Execute a smooth pass when the timing is right.  Count how many seconds it takes to complete the pass.

## Exercise 10 – Freeway - Rural

When you encounter a traffic pulse in a rural area, perfect your rural freeway advancement.  The traffic will invariably merge into the left lane well in advance of the pass.  Stay in the right lane to pass, use your merging skills to reenter the left lane and complete the pass of the vehicle in the right lane.  Then merge back to the right.  Repeat as needed.

## *Quiz*

Test your knowledge of the material covered in this volume.
Select all that apply.

1. What is the most critical factor in successfully
   negotiating a regular commute?
       A. The psychology of the average commuter
       B. The vehicle you drive
       C. Good weather
       D. Good rearview mirrors
2. When are the most consistent driving patterns evident?
       A. Afternoons on weekends
       B. The morning commute
       C. Late at night
       D. During lunch hour
3. Select all that are primary factors in a commute:
       A. Where do you have to go?
       B. How far is it?
       C. Is my coffee shop on my primary route?
       D. How long do I need to be there?
4. What is the recommendation for determining the
   dimensions of your vehicle?
       A. Take a photo of your vehicle and put it on the
          dashboard.
       B. Ask your passenger if you're too close.
       C. Go to a large empty parking lot and pull your
          vehicle up to a light post or other similar object
          and make sure you can pull all of the way up to
          it without touching; both forwards and
          backwards.
       D. Hang a tennis ball from the ceiling of your
          garage so you can tell when you're close
          enough.

5. How can you determine the psychology of drivers around you?
    A. Honk at them and see how they react.
    B. Make an obscene gesture and see how they react.
    C. Observe their behavior; determine their driver profile.
    D. Tailgate them and see if they speed up.
6. Which Driver Profiles are the best to follow?
    A. Office Worker Male and Salesperson
    B. Tailgater and Macho Driver
    C. Delivery Truck Driver and Angry Driver
    D. Construction Supervisor and Observant Driver
7. Select all of the identified Subconscious Driving Patterns:
    A. Subconscious Overtaken Reaction
    B. Subconscious Merge Reaction
    C. Texting While Driving
    D. Go Fast and Then Slow
    E. Leader of the Pack
    F. False Sense of Slowing
    G. Standard Start Gap
8. Select all of the identified Conscious Driving Patterns:
    A. Inconsiderate
    B. Usual
    C. Psychopathic
    D. Righteous Driver
9. How should you deal with your psychology during your commute?
    A. Know that every day you will need to deal with a new set of circumstances that will improve your driving skills.
    B. Think of your commute as a race.
    C. Absorb yourself in an audiobook.
    D. Schedule back-to-back conference calls.
10. Select the identified Driving Environments:

A. City Multi-Lane Roads
B. Traffic Lights
C. Freeway - City
D. Cascading Braking
E. Traffic Accordions
F. Delivery Vehicles
G. Weather
H. Freeway - Rural
I. Toll roads
J. Traffic Circles
K. Reversable Lanes

11. What is the most important Driving Skill?
    A. Observation
    B. Effective swerving
    C. Blinker operation
    D. Fine tuning rearview mirrors while executing a merge

12. What is the most important mental Driving Skill?
    A. Forgiving people who cut you off
    B. Maintaining composure when someone is tailgating
    C. Planning
    D. Tuning out the traffic, so you can concentrate on the conference call

13. What is the most critical of the actual Driving Skills?
    A. Passing
    B. Merging
    C. Tailgating
    D. Connecting your Bluetooth devices

14. It is possible to merge into a lane where the traffic is stopped.  T / F

15. If you hesitate on a merge, what is likely to happen?
    A. The vehicles in the adjacent lane will back-off and let you merge
    B. The vehicles in the adjacent lane will move-up to prevent your merge

    C.   The vehicles in the adjacent lane are unlikely to notice during rush hour

    D.   The vehicles in the adjacent lane will move ahead of you and merge into your lane

16. What is the usual cause of Cascading Braking?

    A.   An improper lane change ahead

    B.   An accident

    C.   A stalled vehicle

    D.   Too many vehicles on the road

17. The most consistent traffic advancement opportunities in multi-lane freeway commuting are usually due to:

    A.   Following a tailgater

    B.   Driving in the fast lanes

    C.   Staying in the same lane all the way

    D.   Traffic accordions

18. An advanced traffic advancement technique, the diagonal maneuver, is a technique where you:

    A.   Take advantage of the different speeds the traffic accordion opens and closes – merging diagonally.

    B.   Look down the road diagonally for other advancing cars.

    C.   Make a stutter movement with your vehicle before you exit.

    D.   Make a braking action used while changing lanes.

19. During heavy traffic, on a multi-lane city freeway, which lane will typically advance the fastest?

    A.   Lane 1 – Carpool lane

    B.   Lane 2 – The Fast Lane

    C.   Lane 4 – The second lane from the right or Truck Lane

    D.   Lane 5 – The Prepare to Exit Lane

20. When coming to three lanes of traffic stopped a traffic light, which lane should you select?

    A.   The left lane

B.  Any lane without a large truck
C.  The lane with the fastest looking cars
D.  The shortest lane

21. If you know the right lane ends in two miles you should merge left:
    A.  One mile before the lane ends
    B.  Half a mile before the lane ends
    C.  A quarter of a mile before the lane ends
    D.  As the lane ends

22. On an open roadway, after you pass, you should:
    A.  Stay in the lane you're in
    B.  If possible, merge another lane to the left
    C.  Merge right
    D.  It doesn't matter

23. Select all of the ways, listed below, that you as a driver can use to subconsciously affect other drivers to behave in predictable ways:
    A.  Encourage the feeling of top of the hill
    B.  Encourage a leader of the pack
    C.  Encourage a feeling of a false sense of slowing
    D.  Encourage a driver to slow by tailgating

24. Once you reach passing speed, about how long does it take to pass a car on a two-lane highway?
    A.  3 Seconds
    B.  22 seconds
    C.  18 seconds
    D.  6 seconds

25. On a rural freeway, a traffic pulse phenomenon occurs when a __________ passes another vehicle and fails to merge back into the right lane.  The way to get around this traffic pulse is to ____________.
    A.  van, wait until they merge right
    B.  slow vehicle, pass on the right
    C.  state trooper, wait until the trooper exits
    D.  tailgater, tailgate the tailgater

26. While driving in town, you feel that another driver is following you, you should:
    A.   Drive as fast as you can to get away
    B.   Motion the driver to the side of the road, so you can have a word with him
    C.   Pull out your pellet gun and wave it at him
    D.   Drive to the nearest police of fire station
27. Select some of the identified Driving Sins you should not commit:
    A.   Staying left after passing
    B.   Trying to merge into a lane that is stopped
    C.   Preventing others from passing
    D.   Rubbernecking
    E.   Listening to music
    F.   Driving with both feet in a vehicle with an automatic transmission
28. Select some the identified driver's responsibilities:
    A.   Track traffic violators and follow them
    B.   Maintain your vehicle
    C.   Pay Attention
    D.   Contribute to the Free Flow of Traffic
    E.   Know where you're going
    F.   Don't Get Angry

Answers:
   1. **A**          2. **B**     3. **A, B, D**      4. **C**    5. **C**    6. **D**
   7. **A, B, D, E, F, G**    8. **B, C, D**      9.  **A**
   10. **A, B, C, D, E, G, H, I, J, K**          11. **A**   12. **C**   13. **B**
   14. **F**          15. **B**   16. **A**   17. **D**   18. **A**   19. **C**   20. **D**
   21. **D**          22. **C**   23. **B, C, D**      24. **D**   25. **C**   26. **D**
   27. **A, B, C, D, F**      28. **B, C, D, E, F**

## *Actual Route Notes*

Over the years I've taken route notes on many of my commutes. Using the following principle: To manage something you must measure it, so I regularly took route notes. Whether my commute changed because I moved, changed jobs or clients, I didn't keep many of my route notes. I'm including what I have here so that you may either be inspired to do something similar, or hopefully one of these is your commute and these notes may help you.

**Actual notes taken on various commutes**

**Traffic Light Count on Ocean Blvd to PCH**

| | |
|---|---|
| Downtown Long Beach | 20 |
| 2nd Street | 12 |
| Naples | 6 |
| Seal Beach | 6 |
| Huntington Harbor | 5 |
| Bolsa Chica | 1 |
| Huntington Beach | 13 |
| Newport Beach (to 55) | 5 |
| Newport Beach (from 55 to Avocado) | 8 |
| **Total** | **76** |

**Time from Dana Point to Long Beach, CA on PCH to Ocean Blvd**

| | |
|---|---|
| Dana Pt. | 8:52 PM |
| | 8:59 |
| | 9:04 |
| | 9:12 |
| Huntington Pier | 9:26 |
| | 9:39 |
| 2nd St, Long Beach | 9:44 |
| Downtown LB | 9:52 |
| **Total Drive Time** | **1:00** |

**Commute Route Advice:**

Newport Beach to I-73
- Newport Blvd N to Main
- Stay right to 15th St
- Then left at 17th St
- Move right and stay until the last light
- Move left for the extra lane as the freeway begins
- Exit at Baker

Driving the Pacific Coast Highway (California SR 1) north from the Costa Mesa Freeway (55) in Newport Beach to Second Street in Long Beach
- Stay in the extra right lane from the 55 near the Hoag Hospital past Superior Ave. where the extra lane ends
- Merge to the left lane as it will generally move more quickly until you approach Brookhurst Ave.
- Use the extra lane till the lane ends
- After the light, stay left to Orange
- Stay in the right to Beach Blvd.
- Merge all the way left
- Use the extra right lane past Maine St.
- Merge all of the way left to about 17th St.
- Merge right though the Bolsa Chica Wetlands.  Stay in the right lane to Warner
- Merge left at Fifth Street in Seal Beach
- Stay in right lane to Second Street

## *Index*

9 798451 452820